Culture and Cruelty in Nietzsche, Dostoevsky, and Artaud

Culture and Cruelty in Nietzsche, Dostoevsky, and Artaud

Max Statkiewicz

LEXINGTON BOOKS
Lanham • Boulder • New York • London

Published by Lexington Books
An imprint of The Rowman & Littlefield Publishing Group, Inc.
4501 Forbes Boulevard, Suite 200, Lanham, Maryland 20706
www.rowman.com

6 Tinworth Street, London SE11 5AL, United Kingdom

Copyright © 2020 by The Rowman & Littlefield Publishing Group, Inc.

All rights reserved. No part of this book may be reproduced in any form or by any electronic or mechanical means, including information storage and retrieval systems, without written permission from the publisher, except by a reviewer who may quote passages in a review.

British Library Cataloguing in Publication Information Available

Library of Congress Cataloging-in-Publication Data

ISBN 9781793603920 (cloth)
ISBN 9781793603944 (pbk)

For Grażyna Sonia

> Everything that aims at attenuating the cruelty of the truth, at attenuating the harshness of the real, has the unavoidable consequence of discrediting the most brilliant of endeavors or the worthiest of causes.—Clément Rosset, *Joyful Cruelty*[1]

Faust:
Nun gut, wer bist du denn?
Mephistopheles:
Ein Teil von jener Kraft,
Die stets das Böse will und stets das Gute schafft
—Goethe *Faust*[2]

NOTES

1. Rosset, *Joyful Cruelty*, 70; *Le principe de cruauté*, 7: *Tout ce qui vise à atténuer la cruauté de la vérité, à atténuer les aspérités du réel, a pour conséquence immanquable de discréditer la plus géniale des entreprises comme la plus estimable des causes.*

2. (lines 1335–1337): (my translation) Faust: Well, who are you then? Mephistopheles: Part of this force that always wants evil, and always works the good.

Contents

Abbreviations of Nietzsche's Works	xi
Abbreviations of Dostoevsky's Works	xiii
Acknowledgments	xv
Introduction	1
1 Cruelty: Nietzsche's Genealogy of Culture	11
2 "Feeling of Thought": Nietzsche's Critique of Terrible Abstractedness and Dostoevsky's Triumph in the Concrete	39
3 Purification of Cruelty in Antonin Artaud	59
Conclusion	91
Bibliography	95
Works to Consult	109
Index	111
About the Author	119

Abbreviations of Nietzsche's Works

BT	*The Birth of Tragedy and Other Writings* (1871) Trans. Ronald Speirs. CUP, 1999.
UM	*Untimely Meditations* (1873–76) Trans. R. J. Hollingdale. CUP, 1997.
HAH	Human All Too Human (1878) Trans. R. J. Hollingdale. CUP, 1996.
DB	*Day Break: Thoughts on the Prejudices of Morality.* (1880) Trans. R. J. Hollingdale. CUP, 1997.
GS	*The Gay Science* (1882) Trans. Josephine Nauckhoff. CUP, 2001.
Z	*Thus Spoke Zarathustra.* (1883–85) Trans. Thomas Common, Prometheus Books, 1993. *Thus Spoke Zarathustra.* Trans. Adrian del Caro. CUP, 2006.
BGE	*Beyond Good and Evil* (1886) Trans. Judith Norman. CUP, 2002.
GM	*On the Genealogy of Morals and Ecce Homo.* (1887) Trans. Walter Kaufmann and R. J. Hollingdale, Vintage Books, 1989. *On The Genealogy of Morality.* Trans. Carol Diethe. CUP, 2017.
TI	*Twilight of the Idols.* (1881) Trans. Duncan Large. OUP, 1998.
AC EH TI	*The Anti-Christ, Ecce Homo, Twilight of the Idols and Other Writings.* (1888) Trans. Judith Norman, CUP, 2005.
PTG	*Philosophy in the Tragic Age of the Greeks.* Trans. Marianne Cowan, Regnery Publishing, Inc., 1962.

WP	*The Will to Power.* Trans. Walter Kaufmann and R. J. Hollingdale. Vintage Books, 1968.
WLN	*Writings from Late Notebooks.* Trans. Kate Struge. CUP, 2003.
KS	*Kritische Studienausgabe*, in 15 Bänden. Ed. Giorgio Colli und Mazzino Montinari, de Gruyter, 1967–77.
PN	*The Portable Nietzsche.* Trans. Walter Kaufmann, Viking Penguin, 1954.
BWN	*Basic Writings of Nietzsche.* Trans. Walter Kaufmann, The Modern Library, 1966.
BKG	*Briefwechsel, Kritische Gesamtausgabe.* Berlin: Walter de Gruyter, 1981.
B	*Briefe*
DWM	*Der Wille zur Macht.* Alfred Kröner Verlag, 1996.

Abbreviations of Dostoevsky's Works

DW	*The Diary of a Writer*. Trans. Boris Brasol. Charles Scribner's Sons, 1949.
ДП	*Дниевник Писателя*. ЭКСМО, 2011.
GSWFD	*Great Short Works of Fyodor Dostoevsky*. Ed. Ronald Hingley. Perennial Classics, 1968.
CC	*Собрание Сочинечий в десяти томах*. Государственное Издательстбо Художестбенной Литературы.
BK	*The Brothers Karamazov*. Trans. Richard Pevear and Larrisa Volokhonsky. Farrar, Straus and Giroux, 1990.
БК	*Братья Карамазобы*. Эксмо, 2006.
NU	*Notes from Underground*. Trans. Richard Pevear and Larrisa Volokhonsky. Vintage Books, 1993.
ЗП	*Записки из Подполья*. АСТ Астрель, 2006.
D	*Demons*. Trans. Richard Pevear and Larissa Volokhonsky. Vintage Books, 1995.
Б	*Бесы, Роман в Трех Частях*. ТЕРРА, 2001.
HD	*The House of the Dead*. Trans. David McDuff. Penguin Classics 1985. *The House of the Dead*. Trans. Constance Garnett. Dover INC, 2004. *Notes from a Dead House*. Trans. Richard Pevear and Larissa Volokhonsky. Alfred A. Knopf, 2015.
ЗМД	*Записки из Мертвого Дома. Рассказы*. Собетская Россия, 1983. *Записки из Мертвого Дома*. АСТ Астрель, 2006.

Acknowledgments

I am grateful to my students Regina Chiuminatto, Anna Grelson, Elizavetta Koemets, Jeni Legg, Valerie Reed-Hickman, Anna Redmond, Patricia Ruiz Rivera, Ian Atalla, Michael Becker, Daniel Dooghan, Brent Harlow, Thomas Massnick, Peter Orte, as well as Grażyna Sonia Wasilewska Statkiewicz for discussing with me the project of this book.

Introduction

The word "culture" has many meanings, but apparently one valuation. Culture is universally praised. Let us consider the possible models of culture by providing the most general "cultural" background.[1] The vogue of the notion of culture or civilization, and the attempt to define more precisely these sometimes loosely used value words date since at least the end of the eighteenth century, since the age of the triumphant Enlightenment. Most European languages adopted by then the Latin word *cultura* through the French word *culture*. Paradoxically, the French themselves had eventually abandoned the word *culture* in favor of the word *civilization* by the end of nineteenth century.[2] Antonin Artaud, in his preface to *The Theater and its Double* in 1936, noted the still existing confusion between the two terms: "the distinction between culture and civilization is an artificial one, providing two words to signify an identical function."[3] The loose usage of the word culture might be one of the reasons behind Theodor W. Adorno and Max Horkheimer's questioning the term (and the phenomenon) of culture: "to speak of culture (*Kultur*) was always contrary to culture. Culture as a common denominator already contains in embryo that schematization and process of cataloguing and classification which bring culture within the sphere of administration."[4] Others tried to rescue the term by circumscribing more rigorously its semantic field.

Two main clusters of meaning are usually distinguished in the term "culture." First, an anthropological notion with scientific claims, often associated with the name of E. B. Tylor, who defined culture, in his *Primitive Culture* from 1871, as "that complex whole which includes knowledge, belief, art, morals, law, custom and any other capabilities and habits acquired by man as a member of society."[5] Clifford Geertz, more than a 100 years later notes the persistence of this general view of culture in anthropological studies,[6] and then respectfully dismisses Taylor's definition: "its originative power not denied," it seems to him that it has "reached the point where it obscures a good deal more than it reveals."[7] And what it should reveal most forcefully, according to Geertz, is the essential diversity of cultures as the presupposition of modern anthropology:

> Whatever else modern anthropology asserts—and it seems to have asserted almost everything at one time or another—it is firm in the conviction that men unmodified by the customs of particular places do not in fact exist, have never existed, and most important, could not in the very nature of the case exist.[8]

The respect for the diversity of cultures can thus only be assured in the "hermeneutic" examination of particular cultures. Geertz offers his own "semiotic" definition of culture, based on the tradition of Max Weber and Ernst Cassirer. Culture consists of the humanly produced "webs of significance," which are to be interpreted by an anthropologist.[9] Even though not an experimental science, anthropology remains in Geertz's view attached to the scientific ideal of objectivity. The methodology of the "thick description," in particular, which is able to provide a meaning of the behavior, understandable to the persons outside the culture, in contrast with so-called "thin description," able only to describe the facts of a behavior. Thus thick description, at the same time general and specialized, is aimed at an adequate reflection of the complex cultural reality and at the preservation of the universal humanistic ideal:

> Anthropology has attempted to find its way to a more viable concept of man, one in which culture, and the variability of culture, would be taken into account rather than written off as caprice and prejudice, and yet, at the same time, one in which the governing principle of the field, "the basic unity of mankind," would not be turned into an empty phrase.[10]

What is perhaps most remarkable in Geertz's view is this combination of cultural diversity with a rigorous interpretive methodology. The "basic unity of mankind" remains a postulate of scientific anthropology, and thus, re-inscribes it within the tradition of Enlightenment preserved in spite of any relativistic temptation.[11]

The second cluster of meaning, developed most strikingly by Matthew Arnold's *Culture and Anarchy* in 1869, and already anticipated by Henry Buckle's *History of Civilization in England* from 1857, might be considered, on the contrary, as a strong evaluative manifesto of the Enlightenment ideology of culture and progress. It is true that in his ambitious but unfinished work, Buckle professes to lay foundations for the rigorous science of history.[12] But the writers such as Dostoevsky and Nietzsche will criticize him for his not altogether rational belief in a steady cultural progress and its effects on the contemporary morality. Buckle maintains, for example, that the advance of modern culture in Europe has been marked by a reduction of the rule of physical laws and an ever-growing rule of rational laws. A study of European history shows clearly according to Buckle that war, "this barbarous pursuit is, in the progress of society, steadily declining."[13] Dostoevsky's underground man will have no trouble to show the futility of this belief; this is what should happen "logically," but "look around you: blood is flowing in rivers, and in such a jolly way besides, like champagne. Take this whole nineteenth century of ours, in which Buckle also lived. Take Napoleon–both the great one and the present one. Take North America–that everlasting union."[14] And Nietzsche clearly opposes to it the Heraclitean principle of war (*polemos*), war eternally reasserting itself: "You say it is the good cause that hallows even war? I tell you: it is the good war that hallows any cause."[15]

Arnold, more candidly, takes culture to be an idea and an ideal rather than a collective descriptive concept of modern history: an idea of perfection and an ideal of development for the humanity.[16] In the preface to his *Culture and Anarchy*, Arnold defines culture as "a pursuit of our total perfection by means of getting to know, on all the matters which most concern us, the best which has been thought and said in the world,"[17] and he determines the scope of his essay and its predominantly practical task as setting up the idea of culture that would provide a "great help out of our present difficulties."[18] Arnold's eulogy of culture is actually an apology, a defense against the political thinkers of his day, Mr. Bright and Mr. Frederic Harrison, distant heirs of the Greek Sophists of the fifth century BC Greece, who staunchly opposed political action (*ergon*) to (an empty) talk (*logos*),[19] as well as ancestors of some of the twentieth-century critics of the word (and the phenomenon) of culture, famously caricatured in Hanns Johst's play in the nineteen thirties ("when I hear the word culture, I reach for my Browning (gun)").[20] Frederic Harrison, in particular, sounds like a modern Callicles opposing a modern Socrates[21] in the person of Matthew Arnold:

> Perhaps the very silliest cant of the day . . . is the cant about culture. Culture is a desirable quality in a critic of new books, and sits well on a possessor of *belles lettres*; but as applied to politics, it means simply a turn for small fault-finding, love selfish ease, and indecision in action. The man of culture is in politics one of the poorest mortals alive.[22]

Thus the main and immediate practical upshot of Harrison's critique is the exclusion of men of culture from politics: they should not be "entrusted with power." But Arnolds, just like Socrates in Plato's dialogues—in *Gorgias*, for example, or in *Apology*—doesn't wish to be "entrusted with power," and just like Socrates, he would like to enjoin the members of his community to "know themselves" (Socrates's: γνῶθι σεαυτόν or *know thyself*).[23]

In fact, the notion of culture propounded by Arnold is not the same as the one his opponents, "the disparagers of culture," reject. Its motive and principle is not curiosity or vanity. It is not an elitist conception of "cultural Philistines":

> A smattering of Greek and Latin [. . .] valued either out of sheer vanity and ignorance or else as an engine of social and class distinction, separating its holders, like a badge or title, from other people who have not got it.[24]

On the contrary, integration constitutes Arnold's principle of culture. It is the ideal of perfection of human beings living together. Culture "seeks to do away with classes; to make all live in an atmosphere of sweetness and light."[25] Arnold does not accept the traditional opposition between *logos* and *ergon*, exacerbated in the nineteenth-century political writings, as for example in Marx's exaltation of praxis (most famously in his *Theses on Feuerbach*),[26] as well as among Russian nihilists (*slovo* versus *dielo*; as for example in Alexander Chernyshevsky's *What Is to Be Done*, or Sergey Niechaev's "Catechism of the Revolutionary,"[27] as well as in Dostoevsky's *Demons*. Far from being a purely "intellectual" curiosity,[28] culture constitutes for Arnold an active force of integration and of improvement:

> There is a view in which all the love of our neighbor, the impulses toward action, help, and beneficence, the desire for removing human error, clearing human confusion, and diminishing human misery, the noble aspiration to leave the world better and happier than we found it—motives eminently such as are called social—come in as part of the grounds of culture, and its main and pre-eminent part. Culture is then properly described not as having its origin in curiosity, but as having its origin in the love of perfection; it is a *study of perfection*.[29]

This description is of course the description of Arnold's own view, the view of an infinite perfectibility of human nature, through "rendering an intelligent being yet more intelligent," as Montesquieu, whom Arnold likes to quote, formulated one of the ideals of Enlightenment.[30] Marxist opposition between an interpretation of the world and a transforming action is hardly possible in the case of the good. In a truly Platonic fashion, Arnold seems to affirm an almost direct agency of the knowledge of the good. A true culture would imply a passion for doing good, and eventually, actual doing good.

Culture's true sense as expressed in the phrase "sweetness and light"—which appears at least 26 times in *Culture and Anarchy*, is taken from Jonathan Swift's (1704) "Battle of the Books," a preface added to *A Tale of a*

Tub,³¹ where it represents the ideal of the Ancients. It is not certain on which side Jonathan Swift stood in the battle. In any case, Arnold—writing more than one and half century later—seems to be resolutely on the side of "sweetness and light" of the Platonic ideal of perfection and happiness achieved through the theoretical as well as practical knowledge of the good: "the moral and social passion for doing good."³² And the name of this ideal of infinite perfectibility of human community is no other word than "culture."

But "culture" has also another meaning, which is manifest in the word "acculturation," Foucault's *assujettissment*, ideology, or "political correctness." All these phenomena signal a deteriorating of culture, its waning. Nietzsche and Dostoevsky called it nihilism or indifference, when it focuses on daily advantage and excludes any serious interest in the world. In Nietzsche's words, it is a state of the "last men," the despicable figures which we see in Zarathustra's proem. They are also called ironically "good men" in the third part of *Zarathustra*. The last men or the passive nihilists, as Nietzsche also calls them are present in the contemporary world, so much so that we can talk of the nihilist society. We are not concerned with the moral ideals, but we let ourselves be directed by the lowest ideas of personal advantages. Everything accommodates these ideas: mass media, entertainment, and politics. It is this state of moral degradation that Baudrillard calls the "obscenity of obviousness."³³ Everything is already pre-thought, pre-judged, and pre-scribed. As Jean-Paul Curnier writes:

> *La tentative de conquête de la pensée et de l'action politiques par l'exigence poétique a rencontré depuis un adversaire encore bien plus redoutable sous la forme de la culture comme mode de pacification par la puissance publique des tensions que le système génère et dont il a besoin pour fonctionner.*³⁴

Another word combines the many meanings and one, this time negative, valuation; it is the word "cruelty." Cruelty in ordinary sense of the term marks the outer limit of culture, the barbarism, violence toward the weak. There can be physical as well as psychical cruelty, cruelty of enjoying the suffering of others. And yet, in another sense, cruelty could also have a positive connotation, could mean a remedy against the indifference of passive or suicidal nihilism. The supreme form of nihilism is indifference, what Dostoevsky called "indifferentism," and the remedy is precisely the cruelty or difference. Difference is at the center of the thought of Gilles Deleuze. He calls it "difference in itself," it is constituted as this state in which determination takes the form of unilateral distinction. We must therefore say that difference is made, or makes itself, as in the expression "make the difference." This difference or determination *as* such is also cruelty.³⁵ Culture, which ordinarily is opposed to cruelty in a binary way, is more subtly related to it; it marks its genealogy and might be used, as in the case of Dostoevsky, Nietzsche, and Artaud, in its regeneration. It seems wrong to consider culture and cruelty as simple binaries; they are related to each other in a much more complicated way. The focus of this book is on the "positive value" of cruelty the "cruelty of talent," cruelty in art. The main culprit of the degeneration of our culture, which lasts already two centuries according to the dictum of Nietzsche, is not some mythic evil of cruelty, but indifference; cruelty toward animals is the result of that. Difference or cruelty is the only way toward culture's revival. Deleuze and Heidegger explicitly link these both terms. Cruelty marks its genealogy and might be used, as in the case of Dostoevsky, Nietzsche, and Artaud, in its regeneration. In other words, it is not right to consider culture and cruelty as simple binaries, but rather as complementary. The focus of this book is on the "positive value" of cruelty, the "cruelty of talent," cruelty in art. The main culprit of the degeneration of our culture, which lasts already two centuries according to the dictum of Nietzsche, is not some mythic evil of cruelty, but the nihilism of indifference; cruelty toward animals is the result of that. Difference or cruelty is the only way toward regeneration. Deleuze and Heidegger explicitly link both these terms. Hence, the use of them as the most important thinkers of our time.

Deleuze calls the difference cruelty, because it disturbs the orderly view of the world with its classification of genres and kinds (species). Difference in itself is not Aristotle's *differentia specifica* as the principle of definition, which is of the general. It is rather the principle, if we can call it thus, of singularity, of *diaphora* of Nietzsche, or *Austragung* of Heidegger. This difference, first of all applies to art and poetry. Difference is a poetic cruelty in the sense of "making difference," in a poetic (*poiein*—to make, to create) sense.

An ancient text perfectly illustrates this double valuation of human culture and cruelty. It is the so-called *Ode to Man*, or rather to human being (*anthropos*), or, for the classicists, *polla ta deina* ode. The latter transliterate the first words of the *ode*, which are here all-important. They name the double condition of human being: the state of *deinon* (of which *deina* is the plural). "Human being is the most wonderful, but at the same time the most terrible and cruel of living beings." It is the cultural development that makes human being great as Claude Lévi-Stauss will later write. The development of agriculture, domestication of animals, rhetoric, medicine, administration of the cities, all this was the result of the cultural Enlightenment of the fifth-century BC Greece, anticipating the modern Enlightenment.

But Sophocles (the author of the tragedy, *Antigone*, in which this text appears)[36] sees these two aspects of human being, culture and cruelty as inseparable. In fact, one of the translation of *deinon* might be "cruelty." In *Antigone deinon* (wonderful and terrible) points toward Antigone, who says earlier in the play "let me alone and my folly with me, to endure this terror" (παθεῖν τὸ δεινὸν).³⁷ The *deinon* is linked with *atē*—destiny, especially cruel destiny—which Lacan associates with *atroce*.³⁸ Heidegger translates *deinon* as *das Unheimliche* (the uncanny), underlining the double relationship of human being toward home and culture, and the necessity to go through the foreign culture, in a sense of *deinon*, in order to return to one's own.³⁹ *Deinon* marks the tragic nature of human being. It is elevated by its culture, which at the same time renders him/her dangerous to himself/herself and its environment.

The association of *deinon* with Antigone points toward affirmative character of this being.⁴⁰ Cruelty is supposed to resist the cultural emprise of Kreon, the rule of ideological indoctrination of *polis* or community, or the "institutional reality," as John Searle calls it, over feelings and kinship.

The authors of the books on cruelty toward the animals, like Charles Patterson's, *Eternal Treblinka*, Babette Babich's *Words in Blood's*, Gail Eisnitz's, *Slaughterhouse*, point out the nihilistic, industrial treatment of animals, and the cowardice of those who take advantage of these industries, but refuse to directly participate in the slaughter. The call for open cruelty in this case amounts to call for recognizing the immoral aspect of the enterprise. Users of meat, clothing, shoes, upholstery, bags, and so forth should face the cruelty on which the whole industry is based. It is in art that this revelation of cruelty should begin. Three authors, Nietzsche, Dostoevsky, and Artaud share an aesthetic point of view on cruelty. For three of them, cruelty is first of all an artistic principle: "the cruel hammer of creation," of Nietzsche, "the cruel talent" of Dostoevsky's demons, and "aesthetic of cruelty" of Artaud. Camille Dumoulié writes about Nietzsche and Artaud, but the same concerns Dostoevsky: "*Jamais peut-être avant Nietzsche et Artaud l'acte d'écrire, de répandre son encre n'a été métaphoriquement rapproché de l'acte de cruauté, de répandre son sang (cruor), avec une telle insistance.*"⁴¹ It is the manifestation of cruelty that undermines the Enlightenment's conception of human nature and of culture. The culture of "sweetness and light" may be able to overcome the threat of anarchy within the space of Enlightenment, but only by overseeing its cruel aspects. Cruelty, which lies at the roots of all culture and constantly threatens it with annihilation—when revealed, especially in art, literature, and philosophy—radically challenges this very project. Antonio Tabucchi emphasizes this challenge in case of literature: "*La littérature, en substance, c'est cela: une vision du monde différente de celle qu'impose la pensée dominante, ou mieux la pensée qui est au pouvoir quelle qu'elle soit.*"⁴²

Three authors, Dostoevsky, Nietzsche, and Artaud, show the way from philosophical to artistic treatment of cruelty.

The first chapter of the following book is devoted to the work of Nietzsche and its formulation of the threat of nihilism. Nietzsche was also the first to establish the "new opposition," guilty of destroying the ancient tragic culture, namely that of the Dionysian and the Socratic or the Dionysian or the Alexandrian. Nietzsche displaces the opposition from the theoretical to artistic level. The chapter brings together the tragic and the cruel and ends somewhat unexpectedly with the desire of Nietzsche to save the humanity from the threat of cruelty.

The second chapter, in a way compares Dostoevsky to Nietzsche. Nietzsche was only thirty-seven years old when Dostoevsky died. It is nevertheless tempting to study Nietzsche before Dostoevsky. Indeed, Nietzsche's position in the history of nihilism places him, according to Marcel Camus, in the role of the theoretic predecessor of Dostoevsky. Nietzsche "humiliated» reason, that is, "nihilistic" reason, and thus freed it for the "cruel" world of Dostoevsky. The opposition between reason and feeling is at the roots of nihilism. Rational and abstract categories (*Kategorien der Vernunft*) exhibit an excessive attitude toward the world. Nihilism and indifference are the result of this excess. Paradoxically, a violent, cruel challenge toward the categories of reason allows the possibilities of the experience of thought, the feeling of thought.

The third chapter, on the example of Artaud, concludes the way from philosophy to poetry, from nihilism to cruelty, which shows the endeavor of this book. Artaud straightforwardly presents cruelty as a countermovement to established culture. It is good to compare the traditional (Aristotelian) notion of catharsis, which aimed at protecting the limits of dominant culture, to Artaud's "purification," which on the contrary unsettles these limits. The Aristotelian catharsis defended our logocentric culture, whereas Artaudian cruelty shows the downfall of culture and its consequences.

NOTES

1. Or perhaps—as Deleuze would have it—the model of modern culture, on the one hand, and the (anti-)model of a (Nietzschean, nomadic) counter-culture, on the other hand; on the notion of the Nietzschean and of Deleuzean, nomadic, culture, see Deleuze, "Nomad Thought" in *The New Nietzsche*, 142ff.

2. The importance for the development of modern anthropology and studies of culture book of E. B. Tylor, *Primitive Culture* (1871), was translated into French in 1876 as *La Civilisation primitive*. A recent translation of Jacob Burckhardt's (Nietzsche's colleague and teacher) *Griechische Kulturgeschichte* into English as *The Greeks and Greek Civilization* by Sheila Stern testifies to the continuity of this problematic of translation; Nietzsche will attempt sharply to distinguish the two terms on the basis of his view of the two kinds of morality in a note from 1888 (KSA 13, 485), WP, [121] 75: "The high points of culture (*Cultur*) and civilization (*Civilisation*) do not coincide: one should not be deceived about the abysmal antagonism of culture and civilization."

3. Artaud, *The Theater and Its Double*, 8; *Le Théâtre et son double*, 10: *Et c'est artificiellement qu'on sépare la civilisation de la culture et qu'il y a deux mots pour signifier une seule et identique action.*

4. Horkheimer and Theodor W. Adorno, *Dialectic of Enlightenment*, 131; *Gesammelte Schriften*, Band 3: *Dialektik der Aufklärung: Philosophische Fragmente*, 152: *Von Kultur zu reden war immer schon wider die Kultur. Der Generalnenner Kultur enthält virtuell bereits die Erfassung, Katalogisierung, Klassifizierung, welche die Kultur ins Reich der Administration hineinnimmt.*

5. Tylor, *Primitive Culture*, 1.

6. For example in Kluckhohn, *Mirror for Man*.

7. Geertz, *The Interpretation of Cultures*, 4; this definition and the tradition that it generated, has been also criticized in cultural studies as "a rather vague 'complex whole' including everything that is learned, group behavior, from body techniques to symbolic orders" by Clifford, "On Collecting Art and Culture," 66.

8. Geertz, *The Interpretation of Cultures*, 35.

9. Ibid., 5.

10. Ibid., 36.

11. Cf. Denby, "Herder: Culture, Anthropology and the Enlightenment," 55.

12. Buckle, *History of Civilization in England*.

13. Ibid., 137.

14. Dostoevsky, NU, 23; ЗП, vol. 2, 624: *Да оглянитесь кругом: кровь рекою льется, да еще развеселым таким образом, точно шампанское. Вот вам все наше девятнадцатое столетие, в котором жил и Бокль. Вот вам Наполеон,—и великий и теперешний. Вот вам Северная Америка –вековечный союз. Вот вам наконец, карикатурный Шлезвиг-Гольштейн...*

15. Z, I (2006) "On War and Warriors," 33; KSA 4, 59 and 58: "*Ihr sagt, die gute Sache sei es, die sogar den Krieg heilige? Ich sage euch: der gute Krieg ist es, der jede Sache heiligt*"; cf.: "You should love peace as the means to new wars. And the short peace more than the long one" (ibid.): "*Ihr sollt den Frieden lieben als Mittel zu neuen Kriegen. Und den kurzen Frieden mehr, als den langen.*"; for Heraclitus see KSA 1, 825; on the Heraclitean war/desire in Nietzsche, see Land, "Aborting the Human Race," 303–315.

16. Lewis emphasizes the idealistic nature of Arnold's view, which he associates with the whole Romantic movement, of which Arnold would be a continuator: *Cultural Studies*, 86: "As the nineteenth century Romantic poet and scholar Matthew Arnold had insisted, humanism, liberalism and moral improvement were all facilities of *culture* and cultural knowledge: for Arnold and other Romantics "culture" was thus the predicate of refined knowledge and moral purity."

17. Arnold, *Culture and Anarchy*, 5 (viii).

18. Ibid.

19. The classical presentation of this opposition can be found in Plato's *Gorgias* where the "man of action (πράξις or ἔργον)" Callicles opposes the "man of λόγος" Socrates.

20. The famous slogan "when I hear the word culture, I reach for my gun" is a quote from Hanns Johst's play *Schlageter* written in 1933: *wenn ich Kultur höre ...*

entsichere ich meinen Browning ("whenever I hear of culture . . . I release the safety catch of my Browning") act 1, scene 1.

21. See Plato's *Gorgias*.
22. Arnold, *Culture and Anarchy*, 28 (2).
23. Ibid., 29 (3).
24. Ibid., 29 (5).
25. Ibid., 48 (49).
26. Marx, "Theses on Feuerbach," 99.
27. Cf. Benjamin, "The Destructive Character," in *Reflections*.
28. And even "curiosity" does not need to be in Arnold's view a derogatory term for a vain pursuit of superficial knowledge, see his discussion of the term on page 30 (6).
29. Arnold, *Culture and Anarchy*, 30–31 (8).
30. Ibid., 31 (8): "culture is a *study of perfection*," and quoting Montesquieu: "The first motive which ought to impel us to study is the desire to augment the excellence of our nature, and to render an intelligent being yet more intelligent!" *Culture and Anarchy*, 30 (7).
31. "Battle of the Books" in *The Writings of Jonathan Swift*, 385.
32. Arnold, *Culture and Anarchy*, 31 (9).
33. Baudrillard, *Fatal Strategies*, 75; *Les Stratégies fatales*.
34. Curnier, *A Vif*, 18: the tentative to submit thought and political action by the poetical exigency has encountered ever since an adversary still more terrible under the form of culture as a mode of pacification by the public force of the tension that the system generates and which it needs to function (my translation).
35. Deleuze, *Difference and Repetition*, 28; *Différence et répétition*, 43: *[la différence] est cet état de la détermination comme distinction unilatérale. De la différence, il faut donc dire qu'on la fait, ou qu'elle se fait, comme dans l'expression "faire la différence." Cette différence, ou la détermination est aussi bien la cruauté.*
36. Sophocles, *Antigone* [333], in Green edition, 194.
37. Sophocles, *Antigone* [90 and 96] 185; in Loeb edition: "Let me and my rashness suffer this awful thing!"
38. Lacan, *Le séminaire, livre VII: L'éthique de la psychanalyse*, 306.
39. Heidegger, *Hölderlin's Hymn "The Ister"*, 61ff.; *Hölderlins Hymne "Der Ister"*, 74ff.
40. Hegel, *Phenomenology of Spirit*, 284: "But the ethical consciousness is more complete, its guilt more inexcusable, if it knows *beforehand* the law and the power which it opposes, if it takes them to be violence and wrong, to be ethical merely by accident, and like Antigone, knowingly commits the crime."
41. Dumoulié, *Nietzsche et Artaud*, 10: "Perhaps never before Nietzsche and Artaud the act of writing, of spilling ink was metaphorically closer to act of cruelty, to spill blood (*cruor*), with such insistency."
42. Tabucchi, "Éloge de la lttérature" 18: literature, in essence, is this: a vision of the world, different from the one that dominant thought imposes, or better the thought which is in power whatever it is (my translation).

Chapter 1

Cruelty

Nietzsche's Genealogy of Culture

> This same cruelty that we found at the heart of every culture lies also at the heart of every powerful religion, and in the nature of *power* in general, which is always evil.—Nietzsche, "The Greek State"[1]

"The problem of culture in Nietzsche has been underestimated, and yet it forms the origin and center of his thought," wrote famously Eric Blondel.[2] This concerns already the first book of Nietzsche. *The Birth of Tragedy or Hellenism and Pessimism* is the title of the 1886 edition of Nietzsche's first book, originally published fourteen years earlier as *The Birth of Tragedy out of the Spirit of Music*. The new edition was prefaced by a substantial "Attempt at a Self-Criticism." The title page from 1872, with the original title was reprinted as well. Thus, the new edition seems to invite a comparison between the two stages of Nietzsche's thought and—together with the section on *The Birth of Tragedy* in *Ecce Homo* from 1888—it offers a unique perspective on the entire span of Nietzsche's writings on the tragic. I take the new title as the point of departure for discussing Nietzsche's notion of tragic culture, centered in my view on the notion of cruelty, which ultimately undermines all traditional binary oppositions. As a background, I evoke not only Schopenhauer's pessimism of resignation, as traditionally mentioned in this context, but also an extreme example of modern cultural optimism, the notion of "sweetness and light" of Matthew Arnold.

PHILISTINES OF CULTURE AND GOATHERDS

"They have something that they are proud of. What do they call it, that which makes them proud? Culture (*Bildung*), they call it; it distinguishes them from the goatherds," notes Zarathustra at the outset of *Thus Spoke Zarathustra*.³ Overwhelmed by the crowd at the marketplace, when his overman is confused with the tightrope walker—that is to say, when his teaching is confused with entertainment—Nietzsche's Zarathustra appeals to the pride of his listeners, the philistines of culture, who do not want to be taken for goatherds. The philistines of culture belong to the age of Enlightenment progress, with its ideal of "sweetness and light," the ideal of "reasonable" happiness. This is the ideal of the "last men," "last human beings" (*die letzten Menschen*), whom Zarathustra regards as most contemptible—that is, no longer able to have contempt for themselves. "'We invented happiness'—say the last men, and they blink."⁴ The men of culture in the marketplace are proud of their progress on the way toward pleasure and happiness, and they are eager to watch the tightrope walker, who has been announced as their entertainment for the day. They do not wish to listen to Zarathustra's teaching/preaching of the future advent of the "overman" (*Übermensch*); they do not wish to "overcome" (*überwinden*) their "humanity." Zarathustra realizes that perhaps he has lived too long in wilderness, and now can only listen to brooks and trees and talk to goatherds. Do the latter represent the primeval world, which the men proud of their culture (the declining culture, *der überspäten Cultur*) would like to suppress? Do they evoke satyrs, whom in *The Birth of Tragedy* Nietzsche associated with the Dionysian world, and set against the representatives of the modern culture, as the tragic culture? "What does the synthesis of goat and god in the satyr point to? What experience of their own nature, what impulse compelled the Greeks to think of the Dionysian enthusiast and primeval man as satyr?"⁵ Zarathustra seems to rethink this question—the question of tragic culture—when he opposes the last men to the goatherds. The introduction of the figure of the Persian sage in the last section of *The Gay Science*, published in 1882—the book, which immediately preceded *Thus Spoke Zarathustra*—with the solemn words "*Incipit tragoedia*" (here begins tragedy) would point in that direction.⁶

When Nietzsche was writing and publishing his first book, *The Birth of Tragedy*, and then was gradually moving from the profession of the philologist of antiquity to that of cultural critic and to that of philosopher (in his *Untimely Meditations*, and then in the *Human, All Too Human*), the Enlightenment views of culture were current in Europe. Charles Darwin's *Origins of Species* was published in 1859, when Nietzsche was nineteen years old, Matthew Arnold's *Culture and Anarchy* was published in 1869, the year Nietzsche was appointed professor of ancient philology in Basel University, and E. B. Tylor's *Primitive Culture* appeared in 1871 when Nietzsche was concluding and proofreading his first book. Later on, when Nietzsche was writing his *Genealogy of Morals* in 1886, the ideas of progress and of the "sweetness and light" of culture and education were firmly established. So much so that Nietzsche's paradoxical exaltation of cruelty and its combination with the tragic culture could hardly appear as a reasonable intervention in the contemporary discussion over the nature of culture and education. A radical opposition between culture and education, on the one hand, and violence and cruelty, on the other hand, seemed to be the most common assumption of most studies of culture and education in the spirit of scientific progress. Even in the Rousseauistic Romantic reversals, war and cruelty remained the counter-value against which the value of culture has been measured. The binary opposition between the evil of cruelty and the "goodness" of a civilized man or a *"bon sauvage"* was maintained.

One could hardly imagine a more "optimistic" view of human nature and of culture than that of Matthew Arnold in his *Culture and Anarchy*. And one could hardly imagine a more radical challenge to this view than that of Friedrich Nietzsche, presented just a couple of years later in *The Birth of Tragedy*, and then in the whole of Nietzsche's work. One might thus be tempted to oppose Arnold's "optimism" to Nietzsche's "pessimism."

BEYOND PESSIMISM AND OPTIMISM

A supposed opposition between Nietzsche's tragic pessimism, on the one hand, and the optimism of cultural progress, which has found its extreme expression in Matthew Arnold, on the other hand, might ultimately be dismissed as a "wretched and shallow chatter" (*das erbärmliche Flachkopf-Geschwätz*),[7] but only from the point of view of those who comprehend themselves in the word "Dionysian," that is to say, those who not only understand the word but are able to experience the state of nihilism.[8] Ivan Soll discusses the problem of pessimism and of Nietzsche's relationship to Schopenhauer and his thought of tragic resignation, which Nietzsche seems to have adopted in *"The Birth of Tragedy out of the Spirit of Music."*[9] Soll distinguishes between three "aspects" of pessimism: descriptive, evaluative, and recommendatory. Even if the last aspect seems redundant (it might seem perverse to appreciate highly a mode of life and at the same time not to recommend it), the distinction between a description of a life and its evaluation sounds reasonable and analytically sound. They neatly place Nietzsche's terminology within a "coherent" system. Soll readily admits that Nietzsche himself might not have appreciated his (Soll's) clear analytical distinction, but that would be at his own (Nietzsche's) peril: "It is in part Nietzsche's failure to draw and maintain such distinctions that obscures his discussion of pessimism."[10] Is this judgment purely descriptive or evaluative? It would depend on the "truth" or "value" of the system of reference. But perhaps the whole dynamic of Nietzsche's thought is to undermine the very possibility of such a system. It doesn't seem that for him, one can describe without interpreting, that is to say, without evaluating, and hence without recommending a course of action. The view of the world depends on our disposition toward it. The position of strength makes any pessimism "pessimism of strength"; the life of suffering is transformed into the life of passion (*pathos*); *Leiden* becomes *Leidenschaft*. To be sure, such transformation requires a "long, brave, industrious, and subterranean" effort, as Nietzsche writes in section 7 of his Preface to *On the Genealogy of Morals*. He criticizes there an indifferent attitude toward the problem of morality, in which the modern man takes into account an aspect of pessimism, but distances him/herself from it. For Nietzsche, on the contrary, nothing is more worthy of being taken seriously than this problematic, and it is this seriousness that will eventually lead to Nietzsche's cheerfulness (*Heiterkeit*), in other words gay science (*fröhliche Wissenschaft*).[11] To be sure, Nietzsche doesn't call this *gaya scienza* "optimism," but in any event this science seems to have largely exceeded any common definition of pessimism. Thus, it is the *refusal* to "draw and maintain" a distinction between the descriptive (or factual) and the evaluative (or interpretative) aspects of life—that is to say, between facts and their interpretation—that constitutes Nietzsche's major break with the traditional categories of Western positivism.[12] Facts are just what there aren't, there are only interpretation.[13]

The notion of cruelty in Nietzsche's writings epitomizes this "long, brave, industrious, and subterranean seriousness" in his dealing with the "gravest question of all" (*die schwerste Frage*), and not only in *The Birth of Tragedy* but in Nietzsche's entire work, namely, the question: "What, seen in the perspective of *life*, is the significance of morality."[14] Indeed, cruelty excludes an indifference to the question of morality. At the same time the development of this notion radically undermines the opposition between the cultural optimism of Arnold's type, on the one hand, and the Schopenhauerian pessimism, on the other hand. It seems also to question a clear-cut difference between the "descriptive" and "evaluative," "prescriptive" kinds of the latter.

Perhaps in the discussion of culture the real opposition, which should be considered, would be that of culture and cruelty. Indeed, it is cruelty that undermines the Enlightenment's conception of human nature and of culture. After all, the culture of sweetness and light may be thought within the same project of Enlightenment. But cruelty, which lies at the roots of all culture and at the same time constantly threatens it with annihilation, radically undermines this very project, as well as the logic of clear and distinct notions such as optimist and pessimist, good and evil, and ultimately that of culture and cruelty themselves.

THE NEW OPPOSITION: TRAGIC CULTURE VERSUS THEORETICAL CULTURE

> Euripides, too, was in a sense merely a mask; the deity who spoke out of him was not Dionysus, nor Apollo, but an altogether newborn demon, called *Socrates*. This is the new opposition: the Dionysiac versus Socratic, and the work of art of Greek tragedy was wrecked on it.—Nietzsche, *The Birth of Tragedy*[15]

It is not likely that Nietzsche had read Matthew Arnold's work; he never refers to it, and he would certainly have referred to a text, the problematic of which is so close to his own. One could, nevertheless, bring together Arnold's discussion of culture in *Culture and Anarchy* with that of Nietzsche in the first of the *Untimely Meditations*. Both diagnose the dire state of contemporary nineteenth-century culture, dominated by opinions and tastes of the middle-class, whom Arnold calls Philistines. And whom Nietzsche calls the representatives of the low or pseudo-culture—"cultural Philistines" (*Bildungsphilister*).[16] But the comparison might become more rewarding (and more sensible) if one *contrasted* Nietzsche's view with that of Arnold's. Nietzsche of *The Birth of Tragedy* and of the second of the *Untimely Meditations* could certainly be included among those "disparagers of culture" who oppose political action to (superficial and mostly abstract and theoretical) culture and whom Arnold criticizes in his book. Thus Socrates and his almost unlimited trust in science as the means of improving the life of individuals and of society appears in both texts, but on the opposite sides. Socrates is the model of the cultural progress for Arnold, and for Nietzsche he is the epitome of the decadent theoretical culture, against which the renewal of tragic culture has to be conducted. To be sure, there are in Nietzsche's texts some attempts to provide a moderate type of "historical culture" and of "aesthetic Socratism," but they will never be able to cover the chasm between the original cruelty of (human) nature and the fragile attempts of reason to render it universally beneficial and "sweet."

An early letter of Nietzsche from April 7, 1866, shows that he was sensitive to the tension between the two worlds, the elemental world of nature and life with their cruelty, on the one hand, and the fragile world of culture supposedly governed by the intellect, on the other hand:

> Yesterday a magnificent storm was in the sky; I hurried out to a nearby hilltop, . . . found a hut up there, a man slaughtering two kids, and his young son. The storm broke with immense force, with wind and hail. I felt an incomparable elation, and I knew for certain that we can rightly understand nature only when we have to run to her, away from our troubles and pressures. What to me were

man and his unquiet will! What were the eternal "Thou shalt," "Thou shalt not"! How different the lightning, the wind, the hail, free powers, without ethics! How fortunate, how strong they are, pure will, without obscurings from the intellect![17]

This is not just a description of the Romantic experience of a sublime storm, but also a reflection on the power of nature in terms of will, and on the attempts to meet them by a sort of sacrifice on the one hand, and an imposition of the human intellectual measure on the other hand. One can see here already an influence of Schopenhauer's language, but also sense Nietzsche's own fascination with the indomitable forces and a desire to join them. Nietzsche will thematize this early experience as the opposition between the modern and the tragic culture.

In *The Birth of Tragedy*, the contrast between the "Dionysian Greek [who] wants truth and nature in their most forceful form," and who transforms himself into a satyr (half man, half goat) on the one hand, and its modern counterpart, an "idyllic shepherd," who is no more than "a counterfeit of the sum of cultural illusions that are allegedly nature," on the other hand, announces the opposition between the health of the authentically Greek "tragic culture" and the modern one in its decline. Contrary to the scientific ideal of modern "theoretical culture," with its standards of exactitude to which it can conform only through parceling off and distancing itself from its object of investigation, tragic culture—which consisted in replacing science (*Wissenschaft*) with wisdom (*Weisheit*)—maintains an intimate relationship with being as a whole, and with nature with all its cruelty.[18] Of the three forms of culture that Nietzsche discusses in this text—Socratic, artistic, and tragic (or, "historically" considered: Alexandrian, Hellenic, and Buddhistic)—the tragic culture is the most difficult to achieve or even to imagine for a modern, theoretical man (Socratic or Alexandrian), who "no longer dares entrust himself/herself to the terrible icy current of being," but is able only to "run timidly up and down the bank."[19] Marked by his/her optimistic view (desire) of the world, a world thoroughly knowable and transformable, s/he doesn't want to face the totality of being (*ganz haben*), with all its questionable character, with all the "natural cruelty of things" (*natürliche Grausamkeit der Dinge*).[20] The terrible stream of becoming, of existence fascinates, but at the same time threatens with destruction the fragile culture of modern theoretical man. Modern art of imitative nature, manifests this fascination and this distress, but is not able to provide a remedy:

> In vain does one depend imitatively (*imitatorisch*) on all the great productive periods and natures; in vain does one accumulate the entire "world-literature" ("*Weltlitteratur*") around modern man for his comfort; in vain does one place oneself in the midst of the art styles and artists of all ages, so that one may give names to them as Adam did to the beasts: one still remains eternally hungry, the "critic" without joy and energy, the Alexandrian man, who is at bottom a

librarian and corrector of proofs, and wretchedly goes blind from the dust of books and from printers' errors.[21]

An increasing systematization of knowledge, dispassionate and uninvolved studies of all cultures, cataloguing books, multiplying commentaries and critical editions, collecting works of art from all periods and from all-over the world, canonizing the so-called world-literature cannot replace a genuine confrontation with existence (*Dasein*), and with its foremost manifestation in the tragic art.

Between the two passages referred here—the fervent affirmation of the possibility of tragic culture (in the form of the Wagnerian musical drama) and the impasse of modern theoretical culture—there is in *The Birth of Tragedy* a famous passage on the future generation of "dragon slayers," the heroes of the tragic epoch, who *would* dare to "turn their back on all the weaklings' doctrines of optimism in order to 'live resolutely' in wholeness and fullness."[22] And Nietzsche asks whether it would not be necessary for an artist of such a tragic culture to conceive of an art as "metaphysical comfort" (*der metaphysische Trost*). This question calls unambiguously for an affirmative answer in *The Birth of Tragedy*. Fourteen years later, however, Nietzsche will answer the same question with a decisive "no." In his "Attempt at a Self-Criticism," he reproduces the passage verbatim and then says:

> No, thrice no! O you young romantics: it would not be necessary! . . . No! You ought to learn the art of this-worldly comfort first; you ought to learn to laugh, my young friends, if you are hell-bent on remaining pessimists. Then perhaps, as laughers, you may some day dispatch all metaphysical comforts to the devil—metaphysics in front.[23]

It is amazing to see Nietzsche so vehemently rebuking here his former, romantic, "Hegelian" and "Schopenhauerian" self, and denying art the function of the aesthetic, metaphysical justification or redemption of the world. Would it be still possible to talk of "tragic culture," a culture that would only reveal (*offenbaren*) its general distress without a temptation to sublate (*aufheben*) it aesthetically? Nietzsche's genealogical analysis of culture seems to be following the lead of this question. Perhaps the world (of culture and of nature) cannot be redeemed, and it is no use to pretend it can, and perhaps life doesn't need to be redeemed, and it would be harmful to pretend otherwise.

CRUEL ORIGINS OF CULTURE

> One should relearn about cruelty and open one's eyes.—Nietzsche, *Beyond Good and Evil*[24]

> How much blood and cruelty lie at the origin of all "good things"! ...
> —Nietzsche, *On the Genealogy of Morals*[25]

Nietzsche's particular interest in the scrutiny of the origin (*Ursprung*) or rather descent or provenance (*Herkunft*) and emergence (*Entstehung*)[26] of modern culture dates from *The Human, All-Too Human*, composed in 1877, as he himself writes in the Preface to *On the Genealogy of Morals*.[27] In the first edition of *The Gay Science*, published in 1882, Nietzsche called for a detailed historical, comparative study of some phenomena that have given "color to existence" such as love, conscience, cruelty, or such cultural institutions as law and punishment.[28] *On the Genealogy of Morals*, published five years after *The Gay Science* (and one year after the new edition of *The Birth of Tragedy*), attempts to answer this call. It presents a new, more nuanced ("gray") view of culture and cruelty. The typology of *The Birth of Tragedy* is not repeated here, but the domestication of the human animal surely contains the elements of the scholarly Alexandrian culture. And it is again the attitude toward cruelty that serves as the criterion of the development of human culture. The second essay of this work in particular points to the instinct of cruelty as the principle of life (*cruor, cruoris* in Latin means blood, gore, and also murder and slaughter) and to its turning against itself as the origin of conscience (in particular bad conscience), the source of any cultural institution. "Cruelty is there exposed for the first time," writes Nietzsche one year later in the section on *Genealogy* in *Ecce Homo*, "as one of the most ancient and basic substrata of culture that simply cannot be imagined away."[29] Culture and cruelty are here strongly—one might say provocatively—associated. *Genealogy of Morals* is after all a *Streitschrift*, a polemic. And it is against the view of a progressive separation of culture and cruelty, against the ultimate purification of culture, and of Progress by capital "P" in the ideology of the Enlightenment, that Nietzsche is directing his polemic.

The polemic force of Nietzsche's essay depends to a large extent on the ambivalent nature of the notion of cruelty. It is true that all words are like pockets or bags (*Taschen*), "into which now this, now that, now several things at once have been put!" according to aphorism 33 of "The Wanderer and His Shadow."[30] Cruelty is nevertheless a *Tasche* in an eminent sense. Nietzsche sometimes refers to the common cultural rejection of such manifestation of cruelty as vivisection (*Thierquälerei*), paradoxically considered a "beastly" behavior.[31] This phenomenon might be part of what he calls the "barbarian" Dionysian in *The Birth of Tragedy*: "the horrible 'witches brew' (*Hexentrank*) of sensuality and cruelty."[32] In *The Gay Science*, in the aphorism 73 (Holy Cruelty), people reproach a holy man his cruelty when he recommends a murder of a deformed child.[33] In *Thus Spoke Zarathustra*, Zarathustra evokes with repugnance the cruelty of the soul in regard to the body and in regard to itself within the dominant metaphysical and religious tradition of the West.[34] This is also the meaning and value given to this word by the representatives of the spirit of revenge in section 7 of the First Essay in *On the Genealogy of Morals*, when—considering themselves "the good"—they call the powerful "the evil" (*die Bösen*) and "the cruel" (*die Grausamen*); they want them to be "in all eternity the unblessed, accursed, and damned."[35] This is also the meaning of Nietzsche himself in the next section, where the "ghastly paradox of the 'God on the cross'" is qualified as "an unimaginable ultimate cruelty."[36] In the second book, in section 23, when concluding the discussion of the "will to self-tormenting" (*Wille zur Selbstpeinigung*) and "repressed cruelty" (*zurückgetretene Grausamkeit*) of section 22, Nietzsche seems to point again to the ordinary notion of "cruelty," but remarkably in the concluding section 24, he no longer uses the key-word *Grausamkeit*, but a more specific term for cruelty to animals or animal torture: "We modern men are the heirs of the conscience-vivisection (*Gewissens-Vivisektion*) and self-animal torture (*Selbst-Thierquälerei*) of millennia: this is what we have practiced longest, it is our distinctive art perhaps, and in any case our subtlety in which we have acquired a refined taste."[37]

It is this genealogical analysis of the cruel origins of modern culture, and of its constant cruel component, that gained Nietzsche the title of the prophet of our epoch among most of the readers of *On the Genealogy of Morals*. Babette Babich, for example, in her *Words in Blood, Like Flowers*, reads Nietzsche's text as anticipating/provoking such contemporary critiques of our culture of cruelty as Gail Eisnitz's *Slaughterhouse*, Charles Patterson's *Eternal Treblinka*, or Shiv Visvanathan's "On the Annals of the Laboratory State."[38] To be sure, Babich is focusing on the "literally" cruel aspects of our culture, present in the slaughterhouses of the meat industry, in hunting, fishing, vivisection, and so forth, on which we depend in our everyday life: "we eat and we drink, we wear and we shod with, we sleep upon, and we play with the artifacts of death."[39] As to the "self-cruelty" (*Gewissens-Vivisektion* and *Selbst-Thierquälerei*), the source of bad conscience, Babich's book functions in an exemplary way: "Forgive me for these examples."[40] We, human beings of the twenty-first century "universal" culture, shouldn't be disturbed by cruel images. But let us remember, *Grausamkeit* is for Nietzsche a "pocket-word."

Indeed, in the same text—the second essay of *On the Genealogy of Morals*—the word "cruelty" receives an altogether different acceptation. In section 11, it becomes part of the "highest culture" (*höchsten Cultur*) of "noble races" (*vornehmer Rassen*)—the ancient Greeks for example, as praised by Pericles, or ancient Japanese or Arabian, or Romans, feared by their enemies—and it is associated with war and victory: "the voluptuousness of victory and cruelty."[41] The famous Hesiodic division of one historical/mythical epoch into the "age of heroes" and the "age of bronze" exemplifies the double valuation of men and their acts: glorious and victorious for the heroes and their heirs, but "hard, cold, cruel, devoid of feeling or conscience, destructive and bloody" for those who suffered from those acts: "the downtrodden, pillaged, mistreated, abducted, enslaved" and for their descendants.[42]

It is in the same section that Nietzsche exhibits the ambivalence of this other pocket-word, namely "culture." As opposed to the high culture of ancient Greeks, or ancient Germans, "Goths" or "Vandals," for example, the modern notion of culture refers to the reduction of "the beast of prey 'man'" to a "tame and civilized animal, a domestic animal."[43] In this modern, enlightened view, reaction and *ressentiment* are the "instruments of culture" (*Werkzeuge der Cultur*) par excellence. Thus, another value of culture seems to be active here—a violent counterpart to Arnold's "sweetness and light"—a value that will allow Nietzsche to condemn these domesticating instruments of culture as "a disgrace to man and rather an accusation and counterargument against *'culture' in general*" (*'Cultur' überhaupt*).[44]

The same kind of ambivalent valuation governs the treatment of both culture and cruelty in the second essay of *On the Genealogy of Morals*. In section 3, the "cruelest rites" (*grausamsten Ritualformen*) and "systems of cruelties" (*Systeme von Grausamkeiten*) are condemned, together with "the most repulsive mutilations," as terrible means of creating memory, the condition sine qua non of a compulsory responsibility and thus of the basic legal rules, in other words, culture in the most general sense of the term.[45] After enumerating the old German means of punishment, such as stoning, breaking on the wheel, piercing with stakes, flaying alive, and so forth, through which man finally came "to reason" (*zur Vernunft*), Nietzsche exclaims ironically:

> Ah, reason, seriousness, mastery over the affects, the whole somber thing called reflection, all these prerogatives and showpieces of man: how dearly they have been bought! How much blood and cruelty lie at the bottom of all "good things"![46]

The irony here is not simple, though, as the reminder of the etymology of "cruelty" in this passage, as well as the modification of the semantic field of cruelty through the sections 4–6, indicates. In section 6, Nietzsche proclaims the "ever-increasing spiritualization and 'deification' of cruelty" to be constitutive of "higher culture."[47] And in section 7, he refers with nostalgia to the earlier stages of the formation of high culture, and he challenges the pessimist view of this formation: "let me declare expressly that in the days when mankind was not ashamed of its cruelty, life on earth was more cheerful than it is now that pessimists exist. The darkening of the sky above mankind has deepened in step with the increase in man's feeling of shame *at man* (*die Scham des Menschen* vor dem Menschen)."[48] Shame at man is "expressly" identified as the shame at his/her cruelty. Is this shame a mark of the yearning for the culture of "sweetness and light"? Or is an idea of a kind of "sweet cruelty" conceivable?[49]

It is cruel spectacle—war and festival—that eventually manifests this lack of shame, and calls for a divine approval. The Greek Homeric culture was aware of the importance and even necessity of such spectacle:

> With what eyes do you think Homer made his gods look down upon the destinies of man? What was at bottom the ultimate meaning of Trojan Wars and other such tragic terrors? There can be no doubt whatever: they were intended as festival plays for the gods; and, insofar as the poet is in these matters of a more "godlike" disposition than other men, no doubt also as festival plays for the poets.[50]

Art and poetry might (re-)create the space of cruel spectacle, of which the gods have always been fond. But poets and artists, like the gods, are not only the spectators of the cruel spectacle; they incarnate not only violence, aggression, egoism, the joy of persecution, the cruelty of destruction, but also a desire for creation and formation, for culture in the sense emphasized in the German word *Bildung* (formation). It is true that among the moderns these instincts are mostly repressed. Bad conscience (*schlechte Gewissen, morsus conscientiae*) in particular is an effect of what Nietzsche calls "internalization" (*Verinnerlichung*, cf. the Hegelian *Erinnerung* of consciousness), that is, turning all this energy of aggression and cruelty inward, declaring war against the old instincts, the source of man's "strength, joy, and terribleness."[51] The internalization of cruelty produced an immense inner tension in the soul of human animal opened to a radical transformation of his/her being, making of it "a way, an episode, a bridge, a great promise," rather than the end of an evolution, an "overman" rather than the "last man," in Zarathustra's language.

The dominant mood of *The Gay Science* even after the acknowledgement of the death of God—in fact, since the proclamation of this death by the madman (perhaps because of it)—is elation, an elation of "free spirits," of the "seekers of knowledge"; this is one of the main justifications of the title.[52] A vast sea of heretofore-unsuspected possibilities is open to the explorations of the exulted researchers of new meanings. And the horizon is not so much "terrible" (*furchtbar*) in its infiniteness (*Unendlichkeit*), as it is "finally clear again": "the sea, our sea, lies open again; maybe there has never been such an open sea." To be sure, the danger is readily acknowledged, but it is offset by the necessary "daring of the explorers" (*Wagnis des Erkennenden*).[53] They will have to face a long series of upheavals and destructions; they will need to be "fearless ones" (*Furchtlosen*), as the title of Book Five indicates. Perhaps they will need to emulate the "tyrants" in order to become singular individuals and free spirits, and thus, able to challenge the laws of the dominant culture.

Thus, Nietzsche's notion of culture, doesn't exclude cruelty from its sphere. It rather implies it, as its condition. If culture is to be creative, tragic, it needs cruelty, (*Grausamkeit noth thut*).⁵⁴ Every affirmation of individuality needs cruelty. And culture can only progress through the self-affirmation of the bold individuals, explorers who are not afraid of crossing boundaries. Suppression of cruelty, on the other hand, leads to the domestication of culture, to the culture of the "last man," rather than the "culture of the "overman."

THE GOOD AND THE CRUEL

"In Italy for thirty years under the Borgias they had warfare, terror, murder and bloodshed,—they produced Michelangelo, Leonardo da Vinci, and the Renaissance. In Switzerland they had brotherly love, five hundred years of democracy and peace, and what did that produce . . .? The cuckoo clock."⁵⁵ Harry Lime's (Orson Welles') "Nietzschean aphorism" sounds even more provocative than Nietzsche's own paradoxes. Yet, it is not altogether unfaithful to Nietzsche's view of the cruelty of the historical origins of Western culture.⁵⁶ In *The Gay Science*, for example, in aphorism 23, shortly before the statement of the great tragic dilemma of culture and cruelty in aphorism 26, Nietzsche suggested a re-evaluation of a transition stage in the development of culture, commonly called (and denigrated as) "corruption." He praises the state of corruption (and its manifestation in "superstition") for its "delight in individuality" (*Lust am Individuellen*).⁵⁷ Indeed, undermining the current religious dogma, superstition becomes a "symptom of Enlightenment." It is in this text that "cruelty" undergoes revaluation and is rehabilitated against the common condemnation. Denying Buckle's historical account of the development of modern culture, in which the modes of life become "milder" than in the old, "stronger" religious age, and that it is marked by a drastic decline of cruelty—(*die Grausamkeit ... sehr in Abnahme komme*)—Nietzsche claims that, on the contrary, in this transitional state of corruption, cruelty, which "becomes more refined" (*sich verfeinert*), becomes now also more effective. Especially, "wounding and torturing with word and eye," which are "other kinds of murder," and which accompany the appearance in the time of "corruption" of those human beings whom the Greeks called τύραννοι, a word that is the origin of the modern notion of tyranny. But in Greece τύραννος wasn't necessarily a pejorative term; it just meant a ruler without a hereditary right of kingship (βασιλεῖα). Oedipus was a τύραννος (he was in fact a βασιλεύς but he, and everybody, else except Teiresias, ignored it) and we commonly translate the word in the title of the play as "king." It is such self-made rulers that Nietzsche considers the precursors and the "precocious *firstling instances of individuals*" (*die frühreifen Erstlinge der Individuen*).⁵⁸ Thus the tyrants are for Nietzsche the first real "in-and-for-themselves" (*An-und Für-sich's*), that is to say, first individuals. He doesn't mention Oedipus here, but he does mention Caesar and Napoleon as the models of modern conquering individuality, the "spiritual colonizers" and political creators.⁵⁹ The aphorism 266 in Book 3 of the *Gay Science* eminently apply to those tyrants in the age of "corruption," but also to all striving individuals in any age; it is in them that "cruelty is needed" (*Grausamkeit noth thut*).⁶⁰ This ideal of striving individuals will eventually become the origin of the idea of "overman" in *Thus Spoke Zarathustra*, the measure for human being as "something that must be overcome." In the section "On the Passions of Pleasure and Pain," in the First Part of *Thus Spoke Zarathustra*—continuing the theme of the self-overcoming of the human being, crossing the bridge to the overman—Zarathustra discusses the case of the danger of having multiple virtues: one can become a "battle and battlefield of virtues."⁶¹ Even if war and battle are evil (*böse*), he maintains, it is a necessary evil (*nothwendig ist diess Böse*), the evil beyond good and evil.

"Evil" is the word, which often appears in the proximity of the word "cruelty" in Nietzsche's writings. Part of the famous title, it is associated with Nietzsche's name and thought. In *On the Genealogy of Morals*, when commenting on this title at the conclusion of the First Essay, Nietzsche emphasizes its provocative nature by calling the title *Beyond Good and Evil* a "dangerous slogan," and states that whatever it means, it "does *not* mean 'Beyond Good and Bad.'"⁶² Both these oppositions are principles of valuation but conducted from different perspectives, in fact the opposite perspectives of the slave and that of the master, respectively. "Good" is a quintessentially ambivalent "pocket-word" depending of its opposing value: "evil" or "bad." The former, German *böse*, just like "cruel" (*grausam*) expresses the resentment of the weak toward their masters, the strong, who are hard, tough, unyielding, uncompromising, who are not "nice." "Bad" expresses the contempt of the strong toward the weak. The German word *schlecht* is here more explicit; it is akin to the word *schlicht* (plain, simple, common).⁶³ *Schlecht* or bad indicates the low level in the hierarchy of values from the point of view of nobility. As Nietzsche says in aphorism 260 of the *Beyond Good and Evil*, "the opposition of 'good' and '*bad*' means, within this type of morality, approximately the same as 'noble' (*vornehm*) and 'contemptible' (*verächtlich*)."⁶⁴

The opposition between "good" and "evil" governs another type of valuation, another type of morality. The "evil" (*böse*) is the name given to those who are strong, powerful, masterful—those who call themselves "good" in the first type of evaluation—by the weak, who are dominated, that is to say, those who are called "bad" in this first type. The latter call themselves "good" because of suffering and empathizing with the suffering: the poor, the unhappy, the wretch. The virtue of selflessness is the measure of this type of valuation of morality. And it is from this point of view that "the evil, the cruel, the lustful, the insatiable," are condemned as "the godless to all eternity," "the unblessed, accursed, and damned."[65] In the title and the book *Beyond Good and Evil* Nietzsche rejects this type of valuation, but in another move he defies its language by adopting and revaluating its two main terms of opprobrium: the "evil" and the "cruel." It is in association with "cruel" that "evil" receives a positive acceptation. In *Ecce Homo*, Nietzsche situates himself, his thought, in the history of "the struggle of good and evil" (*der Kampf des Guten und des Bösen*).[66] Original Zarathustra, Persian sage, who had the courage to face the truth and who knew how to "*shoot well with an arrow*" (*gut mit Pfeilen schiessen*) is Nietzsche's ancestor, and Nietzsche's hero, because he was the first to take up the gravest question, that is, to situate "the struggle of good and evil" within the "machinery of things," the first to have thought morality in terms of metaphysics "as force, cause, goal in itself."[67] It is only natural that Zarathustra himself should be the first to recognize this "fateful error of morality." Nietzsche calls this type of necessity the "self-overcoming of moralists into their opposite," and he adds with emphasis "*into me*."[68] Thus Zarathustra and Nietzsche would be two figures situated on the opposite poles of the fateful development of the gravest question.[69] And Zarathustra, Nietzsche's Zarathustra, is called a "friend of the evil" (*Freund der Bösen*), first by an unidentified character in *Thus Spoke Zarathustra*,[70] and then directly by Nietzsche in *Ecce Homo*.[71] It is also from Nietzsche's mouth that come the fateful words of Zarathustra who affirms that "whoever wants to be a creator in good and evil first has to be a destroyer and smash values," and that "the highest evil (*das höchste Böse*) belongs to the highest good (*höchsten Güte*)," because it is the "creative one (*die schöpferische*)."[72] In order to create in good and evil, one has to conceive of evil not so much as opposed to "good," as opposed to revengeful, resentful, "reactive," in other words, as opposed to a reactive notion of "opposition," and thus, as creative affirmation.[73] The notion of cruelty in *Thus Spoke Zarathustra* will epitomize the violent, "evil" nature of this affirmation.

THE CRUELTY OF THE HAMMER

It seems that Nietzsche not only recommended to philosophize with a hammer, he recommended to make art with hammer as well. It is in this sense of affirmation that Nietzsche talks about "hammer blows" of artists and their "artists' violence" in section 17 of the second essay of *On Genealogy of Morals*. In section 18, he proclaims the self-ravishment (*Selbst-Vergewaltigung*) of those with an "*active* 'bad conscience'" and the "artists' cruelty" (*Künstler-Grausamkeit*) to be the "womb of all ideal and imaginative phenomena," as well as the source of "an abundance of strange new beauty and affirmation, and perhaps beauty *tout court* (*die Schönheit*)."[74] Thus at the end of the long analysis—a genealogical analysis—of the essential aspects of modern culture, Nietzsche's conclusion presents cruelty not only as the condition of culture, as necessary evil, but also as its creative, life-affirming power. Both art and philosophy ("new metaphysics")—the driving forces of culture—are unthinkable without "terrifying seriousness." It is not an accident that the conclusion of the second essay of the *Genealogy* sends us to the figure of Zarathustra. For the conclusions of the analysis in *On the Genealogy of Morals* was not a new discovery for Nietzsche, but only a genealogical confirmation of his tragic philosophy and of cruelty as the principle of life and art.[75]

When in the opening section of the second part of *Thus Spoke Zarathustra*, Nietzsche presents his title character in the context of artistic creation, he might be recalling the experience of a storm that he described in a letter from 1867.[76] Zarathustra, pregnant with wisdom is about to descend to his friends (and his enemies); he appears as a "seer" (*Seher*) and a "singer" (*Sänger*). His inspiration comes to him "like a storm" (*wie ein Sturmwind*). He is impatient with the slowness of ordinary speech, and challenges nature, the storm directly: "I leap into your chariot, storm! And I shall whip even you with the whip of my malice" (*mit meiner Bosheit*).[77] This instance of a sublime rapturous merging with nature is an experience of "creating will" (*schaffender Wille*). In the following section Zarathustra returns to the human world, and to the image of an apparently Apollonian artist, a sculptor: "I am always driven anew to human beings by my ardent will to create; thus the hammer is driven towards the stone."[78] But then the relationship between the artist and its material becomes more ambiguous: "in the stone sleeps an image, the image of my images! A shame it must sleep in the hardest, ugliest stone!" An inert resistance of the "stone" requires an uncommon cruelty from the artist: "Now my hammer rages cruelly against its prison. Shards shower from the stone: what do I care?"[79] The cruelty of nature is here matched by the cruelty of human art. The cruel hammer of the artist should create the overman ("you could well create the overman . . . this shall be your best creating!") and the world ("what you called world, that should first be created by you").[80] But ultimately the overman and his world are images of the artist liberated from the prison of the stone, the image of images, the creating will, eventually the will to will, the self-affirmation and self-overcoming.[81] The view of the cruelty of creation is finally reaffirmed in section 8 of the second book of *Thus Spoke Zarathustra*. The "famous wise men" of the title are depicted as servile to the dominant opinion and to the powers that be; they serve ideology rather than truth. They only pretend to don the lion skin, "the skin of the predator, and the mane of the explorer, the searcher, the conqueror!"[82] Only the free spirits, "hungry, violent, lonely, godless . . . feared and fearsome" have the right to claim the "lion-will" (*der Löwen-Wille*).[83] Zarathustra characterizes spirit as "life that itself cuts into life," that is to say, as self-cruelty of creation. Creation requires sacrifice from the artist him/herself: the happiness of the spirit is "to be anointed and through tears to be consecrated as a sacrificial animal."[84] The creative spirit, the builder is the "anvil" and the hammer of creation, even though the cruelty of his artistic process, the "cruelty of the hammer" (*die Grausamkeit seines Hammers*) is not readily visible.[85] In the third book, Zarathustra himself is figured as a stone, subordinated to the spirit of gravity, his archenemy, who proclaims:

> "Oh Zarathustra" . . . "You stone of wisdom! You hurled yourself high, but every hurled stone must—fall!
> Oh Zarathustra, you stone of wisdom, you sling stone, you star crusher! You hurled yourself so high—but every hurled stone—must fall!
> Sentenced to yourself and to your own stoning; oh Zarathustra, far indeed you hurled your stone—but it will fall back down upon *you*!"[86]

To be sure, it is in this crucial section "On the Vision and the Riddle," that the notion of the circle of eternity is introduced, and thus, the idea of eternal recurrence, the formula of the highest affirmation. It is also in this section that the image of "unexplored seas" as the realm of infinite possibilities for daring and "riddle-happy" "searchers, researchers"—an image that will be developed in Book Five of *The Gay Science* (written several years later)—makes its appearance. But the formula itself, and the cruel image of the shepherd biting off the head of the snake remain a "riddle" (*Räthsel*), and the warnings of the spirit of gravity remain in force.

Finally, the ambiguous character of the cruel Dionysian force is epitomized in the fourth book of *Thus Spoke Zarathustra*, in the image of Dionysius himself, the god of tragedy, who appears in the song of "the Magician" as the "cruelest hunter."[87] If the wailing of the old sorcerer, the main rival of the Dionysian Zarathustra, might appear insincere, this is certainly not the case in another version of this song, "Ariadne's Complaint," one of the *Dionysian Dithyrambs*, and one of the final texts of Nietzsche.[88] It is obvious then that the exaltation of the Dionysian creator is not unproblematic, and it seems that that word "cruelty" in all the formulations of *Thus Spoke Zarathustra*, points toward the notion of the tragic, of which Nietzsche considers himself to be the "discoverer."

CRUELTY OF THE TRAGIC

Indeed, in 1884, the year of the "publication" of the third part of *Thus Spoke Zarathustra* Nietzsche wrote in his note book:

I have presented such terrible images to knowledge that any "Epicurean delight" is out of the question. Only Dionysian joy is sufficient: *I have been the first to discover the tragic*. The Greeks, thanks to their moralistic superficiality, misunderstood it. Even resignation is *not* a lesson of tragedy, but a misunderstanding of it! Yearning for nothingness is a *denial* of tragic wisdom, its opposite.[89]

Nietzsche's claim is striking even within Nietzsche's hyperbolic mode of thinking and writing. Walter Kaufmann remarks this in a note to his translation and explains it by the reference to the history of the interpretation of the Greek tragedy from Plato to Schopenhauer and the non-moralistic view of tragedy expounded in *The Birth of Tragedy* section 7. But it is hardly plausible that Nietzsche would just repeat his previous claim in the text that does not recapitulate his work. And in *Ecce Homo*, in the section ostensibly devoted to such recapitulating interpretation of *The Birth of Tragedy* (in the chapter "Why I Write Such Good Books"), Nietzsche makes a more general claim of being "the first *tragic philosopher*."[90] The two texts are of course not unrelated. What Nietzsche calls the tragic is a certain knowledge, or at least a desire for knowledge of the "terrible and questionable" character of things, a certain perspective on existence, a certain "wisdom" that is not bound to a particular literary form.

In the posthumous note from 1884 Nietzsche is comparing three attitudes toward reality, "Epicurean delight," nihilistic resignation, and "Dionysian joy". But what really counts here is the confrontation, the weighing of the knowledge of reality and its acceptance or denial. And given the "terribleness" of the image of reality, simple acceptance seems impossible, and thus the only possible affirmation of reality would be Dionysian delight. Cruelty is at the same time part of the "terribleness" of the interpretation of reality and of its creative (Dionysian, that is, artistic) transformation. However, if one tries to read this note in aesthetic terms of *The Birth of Tragedy*, the "images" (forms, *Bilder*) seem to appear on the Dionysian side of the Apollonian/Dionysian divide, and "Dionysian joy" on the side of the (Apollonian?) solace. This is all the more puzzling in view of a later note, which seems to confirm the valences of the "original" opposition:

Apollo's deception: the *eternity* of the beautiful form; the aristocratic law that says "*thus shall it be forever!*"
Dionysos: sensuality and cruelty. Transience could be interpreted as enjoyment of the engendering and destroying force, as continual creation.[91]

Again, what results from the juxtaposition of the two notes is the view of the cruel, terrible nature of both the reality and the force of its transformation. Apollo and his realm are still there, but the essential confrontation is that between the cruelty of existence and the cruelty of its transformation in the process of continual creation. The apparent reversal is in fact a "twisting of" (*die Herausdrehung*)—to use Heidegger's expression from his *Nietzsche I*,[92] and which applies to Heidegger himself, rather than to Nietzsche—the metaphysical structure of representation. The notion of purely aesthetic attitude, the aesthetic justification of the world—not only that of "metaphysical solace," explicitly rejected in "An Attempt at A Self-Criticism"—is now equally out of the question. An aesthetic "capital question" (*Hauptfrage*) of the relationship between the Apollonian and the Dionysian elements in art[93] is necessarily transposed into "the gravest question" (*die schwerste Frage*), namely, "what, seen in the perspective of *life*, is the significance of morality?"[94] A "moralistic" attitude is not thereby reintroduced. Rather, the *question* of morality, in the sense of the "morality of custom" or "morality of mores," that is, of traditional, Hegelian culture, seems to be taken into account within the perspective of tragedy. Already in *Daybreak*, Nietzsche equated morality with (no more than) submission to customary rules, that is, to "the traditional way of behaving and evaluating".[95] Nietzsche uses the words *Moral* (or *Moralität*) and *Sittlichkeit* almost interchangeably here (and Hollingdale translate them both by "morality"), but there is a(n) (im)moral thesis in this equivalence, and perhaps seeds of tragic knowledge, namely in the qualification "*no more!*" (*nicht mehr!*), which excludes any transcendental origin of morality, of culture, and doesn't allow for any other redemption (*Erlösung*) than that of tragic, cruel knowledge.[96] Indeed, the gravest question is asked within, and "in addition to," the whole series of questions concerning the origin of Greek culture, perhaps of any great (healthful, youthful) culture, in the "Dionysian madness" (*der dionysische Wahnsinn*)—epitomized in the figure of the satyr, at the same time goat and goatherd—in what is terrifying, questionable, ugly, frightful, evil, that is, cruel in the sense we encountered in *On the Genealogy of Morals*.[97] For "*what is it about himself that the tragic artist communicates? Doesn't he show his fearlessness in the face of the fearful and questionable?*"[98]

Even before a comparative history, that is genealogical investigation, of the phenomenon of cruelty has been completed in *On the Genealogy of Morals*, Nietzsche had formulated, in aphorism 26 of the first book of *The Gay Science*, the tragic dilemma, which seems to mark his thought on the relationship between culture and cruelty, eventually expressed in the "gravest question":

> What is life?—Life—that is: continually shedding something that wants to die; Life—that is: being cruel and inexorable against anything that is growing weak and old in us, and not just in us. Life—therefore means: being devoid of respect for the dying, the wretched, the aged? Always being a murderer? And yet old Moses said: "Thou shalt not kill."[99]

The solemnity of Moses' (or God's) commandment here intimates that even the death of God will not allow for a simple interpretation of (Ivan Karamazov's) "everything is permitted." Any cruel decision will be necessarily a result of a tragic knowledge and choice. An affirmation of suffering and cruelty even against the highest law of culture measures the difficulty of the Dionysian rapture and affirmation. The dilemma of the aphorism 26 formulates a major conflict of Western culture, of any culture: its confrontation with cruelty. Most traditional accounts of the progress of Western culture—often extrapolated to a view of the general development of civilization—places cruelty in the beginning of this development and measures the progress by the degree of the reduction, or even suppression, of cruelty. To be sure, Nietzsche had always questioned this naively optimistic view of the progress from cruelty to culture in the history of the West, as well as the nature of the relationship between culture and cruelty in general. Here in the aphorism 26, the religious culture, namely the Law of Moses, is presented as a guard against murder. But the Law of Moses is ultimately God's commandment, and the readers of the Third Part of *The Gay Science* know that "God is dead." Not only that—s/he knows that God died violently, that it was murder, and that it was *our* deed: "We have killed him—you and I! We are all his murders."[100] Thus, cruelty appears not only at the beginning of a culture, but also at its certain end, its revaluation or at least an opening of such possibility of revaluation. To be sure, it is a madman who says this, but his words are confirmed in *Thus Spoke Zarathustra*, the next book of Nietzsche, by the prophetic voice of Zarathustra himself. The Madman in *The Gay Science* seems to be a prophet himself.[101]

Is the notion of cruelty and murder in the aphorism 26 of *The Gay Science* the same as that which refers to the murder of God in aphorism 125? If so, then cruelty would share the ambivalence and uncertainty of the "destiny of Western history."[102] On the one hand, it seems to open unlimited possibilities; but on the other hand, it is extremely distressing, wiping out the horizon of our understanding. An empty space and cold night of nihilism are threatening.[103]

A murder is at the origin of this distress, and the madman laments the event and wonders at its tremendousness and terrifying nature. Just before the crucial announcement of the death of God in "The Madman," the aphorism 124 entitled "In the Horizon of the Infinite" conveys a certain frustration of the hopes of freedom. It is here that the image of an open sea first appears in *The Gay Science*. But here its infinite openness is terrifying: "there is nothing more awesome than infinity." Nietzsche's "poor bird" (*der arme Vogel*) resembles Kant's dove, flying beyond the air and unable to move in the vacuum.[104] A certain resistance, a certain force of gravity seems to be necessary for any kind of flying or dancing.[105]

THE QUESTION OF TRADITION

Thus the gravest question is also the question of gravity, that is, of the weight of tradition. To be sure, the spirit of gravity is the "deadly enemy" (*todfeind*), "arch-enemy" (*erzfeind*), "ancient enemy" (*urfeind*) of Zarathustra, the dancer, the follower of the bird's way.[106] But, as Nietzsche says in *Human All Too Human* "he who lives for the sake of combating an enemy has an interest in seeing that his enemy stays alive."[107] For without resistance, even a bird wouldn't be able to fly. "One doesn't fly into flying," says Zarathustra the teacher: "whoever wants to fly, someday must first learn to stand and walk and run and climb and dance."[108] And the spirit—also the spirit of gravity—is subject to transformation. In the section "On the Three Metamorphoses," at the outset of the first book of *Thus Spoke Zarathustra,* the strength of the spirit is measured by the amount of weight that, like a camel, it is able to carry.[109] The list of the heaviest burdens for the carrying spirit points toward an estrangement from the reassuring ways of the dominant culture.[110] The spirit of gravity is a guarantor of such accepted ways of behavior. They are protected by the "grave words" (*schwere Worte*) of morality: "good" and "evil."

In this foundational role, the spirit of gravity has obvious affinity with the dragon image within the three metamorphoses of the spirit; Zarathustra presented them at the outset of the series of his speeches.[111] The dragon expresses the traditional morality of duty, the commandment of "thou shalt" ("*du-sollst*"): "'thou shalt' stands in its way, gleaming golden, a scaly animal, and upon every scale 'thou shalt!' gleams like gold. The values of millennia gleam on these scales, and thus speaks the most powerful of all dragons: the value of the things—it gleams in me."[112] This "thou shalt" is challenged by the "I will" (*Ich will*) of the lion. For the function of the lion is to question the traditional values in order to prepare the revaluation and to create new values in the transformation of the spirit into the condition of a child, that is, into creative forgetting and innocence.

The transformation is never complete, though, and there is always a part of the "carrying" spirit of the camel in the lion and of fighting, questioning spirit in a child. As Gilles Deleuze notes the breaks between the three avatars of the spirit are relative: "the lion is present in the camel, the child in the lion; and in the child there is tragic issue."[113] To put it in terms of Nietzsche's note from 1885–1886, quoted above, the Dionysian process of "continual creation" has to combine the engendering and destroying elements, and cruelty is part of each transformation of the spirit. The "Conscientious of Spirit" (*der Gewissenhafte des Geistes*), one of the higher men of the fourth part of *Thus Spoke Zarathustra*, a man for whom honesty consists in being most "venomous, rigorous, vigorous, cruel, and inexorable" (*hart, streng, eng, grausam, unerbittlich*) in matters of the spirit, is in fact a disciple of Zarathustra, and it is quoting Zarathustra when he defines spirit as "life that itself cuts into life."[114] To be sure, the scene with the leeches, might appear as a parody of tragedy, but doesn't Nietzsche of the 1887 Preface to *The Gay Science* suggest a necessary modern transformation of tragedy into parody, and precisely because of the presence of a "malicious" spirit? "*Incipit tragoedia*, we read at the end of this suspiciously innocent (*bedenklich-unbedenklich*) book.[115] "Beware! Something utterly wicked and mischievous (*irgend etwas ausbündig Schlimmes und Boshaftes*) is being announced here: *incipit parodia*, no doubt."[116] One should perhaps think of the ambiguity of the Greek word (and prefix) παρά in the etymology of "parodia": both following the prescription of and "resisting against" the song (ἀοιδή) of culture.[117] This *parodia* would refer in the first place to Zarathustra himself as initiator of the problematic of morality, and then to Nietzsche's Zarathustra, and Nietzsche himself.

Even though Nietzsche had eventually renounced—in "An Attempt at a Self-Criticism"—his previous call for the generation of dragon slayers with their task of bringing a metaphysical solace in modern world, it was certainly not because he had imagined a world without the "dragon" of "*du-sollst*," that is, without a culture of laws and duties. Rather, he might have thought of an acculturation (an indoctrination, *Gleichschaltung*) so successful that any cultural confrontation would need to be a "self-confrontation." Thus the definition of the spirit as life that itself cuts into life might be understood as such inner struggle with the "dragon of culture" that has been internalized not only through the cruel "mnemonics" (*Er-innerung*), through the cruel "instruments of culture" (*Werkzeuge der Cultur*), but also through the action of ideology.[118] If the dragon-slayers belong to the "active voice" of the metaphysics of the subject, the "conscientious of spirit" with his leeches—as well as the camel-hero descending into the swamp of truth (and a genealogist of morals, who can take "*any* truth, even plain harsh, ugly, repellent, unchristian, immoral truth")[119]—belong to its tragic, but also its *par-odic* questioning.

Writing is of course Nietzsche's preferred means of such questioning. It is itself a sort of cruelty. Perhaps not "the sort of cruelty shown by that young Greek god who just impaled the poor lizard," but nevertheless wielding "something pointed," that is, "a pen."(*stilus*).[120] Indeed, the ink of true writing is blood (*cruor*). One has to write "with one's own blood," as Zarathustra puts it in the first part of *Thus Spoke Zarathustra*, in order to experience the cruelty of the spirit ("blood is spirit"),[121] that is again, of life that itself cuts into life. But even this well-established truth of Zarathustra undergoes a *par-odic* questioning, when the same (or is he the same?) Zarathustra of the Second Part disbelieves the value of proving anything with blood: "But blood is the worse witness [*marturos*] of truth; blood poisons even the purest teaching into delusion and hatred of the heart."[122] Is there a contradiction between an exaltation of cruor and cruelty on the one hand, and their condemnation as poisoning the human heart, on the other hand? Perhaps Nietzsche's thought and his writing "does not know contradiction, even when it contradicts."[123] And perhaps the task (and "triumph") of the thought of cruelty in all its shades of valuation—in an individual or in a culture—should be precisely "a violation and cruelty against reason" in other words, against our "logo-centric" culture.[124] And thus it would not be paradoxical to consider as the (desperate) "task" of Nietzsche's life, "*die Aufgabe meines Lebens*," as he says himself in a letter to von Stein, to be the following: "to *take away* from the human existence some of its heartbreaking and cruel character."[125] Paradoxically, questioning the notion of cruelty was an important part of this "task."

NOTES

1. (my translation); KSA 1, Der griechische Staat, 768: *Dieselbe Grausamkeit, die wir im Wesen jeder Kultur fanden, liegt auch im Wesen jeder mächtigen Religion und überhaupt in der Natur der Macht, die immer böse ist.*

2. Blondel, *Nietzsche: The Body and Culture*, 51: *Nietzsche: le corps et la culture*, 79: *La problématique de la culture chez Nietzsche a été méconnue, et pourtant elle constitue l'origine et le centre de sa pensée.*

3. Z (2006), 9 f.; KSA 4, 19: "*Sie haben Etwas, worauf sie stolz sind. Wie nennen sie es doch, was sie stolz macht? Bildung nennen sie's, es zeichnet sie aus vor den Ziegenhirten*"; Geneviève Bianquis discusses the problem of translating *Bildung* and *Kultur* into French in the introduction to her translation of *Unzeitgemässe Betrachtungen—Considération Inactuelles*, 13.

4. Z (2006), Prologue 5, 10; KSA 4, 20: "*Wir haben das Glück erfunden*"—*sagen die letzten Menschen und blinzeln.*

5. BT (1999) "An Attempt at Self-Criticism," [4] 7; KSA 1, Versuch einer Selbstkritik [4] 16: *Worauf weist jene Synthesis von Gott und Bock im Satyr? Aus welchem Selbsterlebniss, auf welchen Drang hin musste sich der Grieche den dionysischen Schwärmer und Urmenschen als Satyr denken?*

6. Higgins makes this clear in her article "Reading *Zarathustra*" in *Reading Nietzsche*, ed. Robert C. Solomon, 137–8.

7. EH (in GM 1989) 272; KSA 6, 311.

8. Ibid., 312.

9. Soll, in *Reading Nietzsche*, 104–31.

10. Ibid., 114.

11. GM (1989) "Nietzsche's Preface," [7] 21; KSA 5, 254–5.

12. See Foucault, "Nietzsche, Freud, Marx," 193–202, in *Transforming the Hermeneutic Context*, 59–69. Cf. Delauze, *Nietzsche & Philosophy*, 1f. *Nietzsche et la philosophie*, 1f.

13. Nietzsche WLN 7[60] p. 139.

14. The question Nietzsche spells out in his 1886 "Attempt at a Self-Criticism," sec. 4, 22 (in BWN); *Was bedeutet, unter der Optik des Lebens gesehn,—die Moral?*—KSA 1, 17.

15. (my translation); KSA 1, 83: "*Auch Euripides war in gewissem Sinne nur Maske: die Gottheit, die aus ihm redete, war nicht Dionysus, auch nicht Apollo, sondern ein ganz neugeborener Dämon, genannt* Sokrates. *Dies ist der*

neue Gegensatz: das Dionysische und das Sokratische, und das Kunstwerk der griechischen Tragödie ging an ihm zu Grunde"

16. UM I, "David Strauss, the Confessor and the Writer," [2] 7; KSA 1, *Unzeitgemässe Betrachtungen I* [2] 165; for Nietzsche's general critique of contemporary "apparent culture" (*Scheinbildung*), and the Christian culture, see Löwitz, *Von Hegel zu Nietzsche*, 326 ff., 393 ff.

17. Middleton, "Nietzsche's Letters and a Poem," in *Reading Nietzsche*, 89; a letter to Carl von Gersdorff from 7 April 1866; "*Gestern stand ein stattliches Gewitter am Himmel, ich eilte auf einen benachbarten Berg, ... fand oben eine Hütte, einen Mann, der zwei Zicklein schlachtete, und seinen Jungen. Das Gewitter entlud sich höchst gewaltig mit Sturm und Hagel, ich empfand einen unvergleichlichen Aufschwung und ich erkannte recht, wie wir erst dann die Natur recht verstehen, wenn wir zu ihr aus unsern Sorgen und Bedrängnissen heraus flüchten müssen. Was war mir der Mensch und sein unruhiges Wollen! Was war mir das ewige 'Du sollst' 'Du sollst nicht'! Wie anders der Blitz, der Sturm, der Hagel, freie Mächte, ohne Ethik! Wie glücklich, wie kräftig sind sie, reiner Wille, ohne Trübungen durch den Intellekt!*"—Nietzsche, *Briefe: September 1864—April 1869*, 121–2.

18. See Kaufmann, *Tragedy and Philosophy*, 296f.

19. *der furchtbar Eisstrom des Daseins*, BT (in BWN) [18] 113 (translation modified); KSA 1, 119.

20. BT (1999) [18] 88; KSA 1, 119.

21. BT (in BWN) section [18] 113–14; KSA 1, 119–20.

22. BT (in BWN) "An Attempt at a Self-Criticism," [7] 26; KSA 1, 21.

23. Ibid.

24. (my translation); KSA 5, 155: *Man soll über die Grausamkeit umlernen und die Augen aufmachen.*

25. (my translation); KSA 5, II, 3, 297: *Wie viel Blut und Grausen ist auf dem Grunde aller "guten Dinge"!*

26. See Foucault, "Nietzsche, Genealogy, History," 76–86.

27. On Nietzsche's genealogy, and his distinction between *Ursprung* on the one hand, and *Herkunft* and *Entstehung* on the other hand, see Foucault, "Nietzsche, la généalogie, l'histoire," in *Dits et écrits I 1954–1975*, 1004; "Nietzsche, Genealogy, History," 76–100.

28. GS I [7] 34; KSA 3, 378–9: *was dem Dasein Farbe gegeben hat*

29. EH (in *GM* 1989) "Why I Write Such Good Books," 312; KSA 6, 352.

30. HAH, vol. II [33] 316; KSA 2, 564: *in welche bald Dies, bald Jenes, bald Mehreres auf einmal gesteckt worden ist.*

31. This is for example the sense given to "cruelty" by Mandalios, *Nietzsche and the Necessity of Freedom*, 89.

32. BT (in BWN) [2] 40; KSA 1, 32: *der Hexentrank von Wollust und Grausamkeit.*

33. GS, II [73] 76; KSA 6, 430.

34. "Oh this soul was gaunt, ghastly and starved, and cruelty was the lust of this soul!"—Z I (2006) "Prologue" [3] 6; KSA 4, Zarathustra's Vorrede [3] 15: *Oh diese*

Seele war selber noch mager, grässlich und verhungert: und Grausamkeit war die Wollust dieser Seele.

35. GM, I (1989) [7] 34; KSA 5, I [7] 267.
36. GM, I (1989) [8] 35; KSA 5, I [8], 269: *die unausdenkbare letzte äusserste Grausamkeit.*
37. GM, II (1989) [24] 95; KSA 5, II [24] 335.
38. See the references in Babich, *Words in Blood, Like Flowers*, 311–12; cf. Spiegel, *The Dreaded Comparison.*
39. Babich, *Words in Blood, Like Flowers*, 139 n. 12; it is here that she quotes Ralph Waldo Emerson: "You have just dined, and however scrupulously the slaughterhouse is concealed in the graceful distance of miles, there is complicity—expensive races,—race living at the expense of race"; for a philosophical discussion of the human/animal relationship from the point of view of cruelty, see Lemm, *Nietzsche's Animal Philosophy*, 34 at passim.
40. Babich, *Words in Blood, Like Flowers*, 138.
41. GM, I (1989) [11] 42; KSA 5, I [11] 275.
42. GM, I (1989) [11] 42; KSA 5, I [11] 276.
43. Ibid.
44. GM, I (1989) [11] 43; KSA 5, I [11] 277; my emphasis.
45. GM, II (1989) [3] 61; KSA 5, II [3] 295.
46. GM, II (1989) [3] 62; KSA 5, II [3] 297.
47. See Kaufmann, *Nietzsche: Philosopher, Psychologist, Antichrist,* 246; for a Christian view of "spiritualization," see Ahern, *Nietzsche As Cultural Physician*, 48 et passim; cf. Fraser, *Redeeming Nietzsche*, 149 f. et passim.
48. GM, II (1989) [7] 67; KSA 5, II [7] 302.
49. See AC EH TI, "Skirmishes of an Untimely Man," [24] 205, on the "drink of sweetest cruelty."
50. GM, II (1989) [7] 69; KSA 5, II [7] 304–5; cf. WP [801] 421: "*sexuality, intoxication, cruelty*—all belonging to the oldest *festal joys (Festfreude)* of mankind, all also preponderate in the early 'artist'"; cf. also an early Nietzsche's preface to an unwritten book *Homer's Contest (Homer's Wettkampf)* in KSA I, 783–92.
51. GM, II [16] 84–5 (1989); KSA 5, II [16] 322–3.
52. One senses an extraordinary feeling of elation in face of both the cruelty of nature and of artistic creation in all of Nietzsche's writings from the letter of 1867 to *Ecce Homo* and *Nietzsche contra Wagner* (from the end of 1888); the thought of eternal recurrence implies more than just acceptance of the sufferings of human existence; it implies the cruelty of a creator who will not weigh the benefits and drawbacks of a particular line of conduct.
53. GS [343] 199; KSA 3, *Die fröhliche Wissenschaft*, 574.
54. GS [266] 151; KSA 3, *Die fröhliche Wissenschaft*, 518.
55. Green, *The Third Man*, 100; the famous phrase was actually added to the script of Graham Green by the actor playing the protagonist Harry Lime, Orson Wells.
56. Cf. Nietzsche's comparison of Cesare Borgia and Parsifal in EH (in GM 1989) "Why I Write Such Good Books" 261.

57. GS [23] 47; KSA 3, *Die fröhliche Wissenschaft*, 395; cf. *KSA* 13, 485.
58. GS [23] 48; KSA 3, *Die fröhliche Wissenschaft*, 396.
59. GS [23] 49; KSA 3, *Die fröhliche Wissenschaft*, 398.
60. GS [266] 151; KSA 3, *Die fröhliche Wissenschaft*, 518.
61. Z, I (2006) [5] 25; KSA 4, I [5] 43.
62. GM, I (1989) [17] 55; KSA 5, 288: *was ich gerade mit jener gefärlichen Losung will, welche meinem letzten Buche auf den Leib geschrieben ist "Jenseits von Gut und Böse"—Dies heisst zum Mindesten nicht "Jenseits von Gut und Schlecht*."
63. GM, I (1989) [4] 28; KSA 5, 261; cf. DB [231] 138; KSA 3, 198.
64. BGE (in BWN) [260] 394–5; KSA 5, 208–9.
65. GM, I (1989) [7] 34; see the discussion of Nehamas in his *Nietzsche: Life and Literature*, 110ff.; cf. Leiter, *Nietzsche on Morality*, 193ff.
66. AC EH TI, "Why I am a Destiny" [3] 145; KSA 6, 367; I shall argue that this struggle refers to the same problematic as the one indicated in Nietzsche's Preface to the 1886 edition of BT ("An Attempt at Self-Criticism," [4]) as the gravest question of all: "What, seen in the perspective of *life*, is the significance of morality?" (in BWN).
67. AC EH TI, "Why I am a Destiny" [3] 145; KSA 6, 367.
68. Ibid.
69. For a discussion of Nietzsche's choice of "Zarathustra" for his hero, see Lacoue-Labarthe's, *The Subject of Philosophy*, 37–56; *Le Le sujet de la philosophie*, 75–109.
70. Z, I (2006) "On Little Women Old and Young," 48; KSA 4, 84.
71. AC EH TI, "Why I am a Destiny" [5] 147; KSA 6, 369.
72. Z, II (2006) "On Self-Overcoming," 90; KSA 4, 149: quoted in AC EH TI, "Why I am a Destiny" [2] 144; KSA 6, 366.
73. For the interpretation of Nietzsche in terms of active/reactive, see Deleuze, *Nietzsche and Philosophy*, 39–72; *Nietzsche et la philosophie*. 44–82.
74. GM, II (1989) [18] 87–8; in *The Case (Fall) of Wagner* (in BWN) and *Nietzsche Contra Wagner* (in PN), we learn that its model is not to be found in Byreuth.
75. Lampert is perhaps right to consider all Nietzsche's books after Zarathustra as preparatory, or perhaps better (at least in the case of *Genealogy*), *confirmatory* of the major and definite theses of *Gay Science* and *Thus Spoke Zarathustra—Nietzsche's Teaching*, 5; cf. Blondel, "Nietzsche: Life as Metaphor," 153: "*the Genealogy of Morals* announces the model of the *Overman* ."
76. See 15 above.
77. Z, II (2006) "The Child with the Mirror," 64; KSA 4, 107.
78. Z, II (2006) "On the Blessed Isles," 67; KSA 4, 111.
79. Ibid.
80. Ibid., 109–10.
81. For a view of the significance of the overman as "the disappearance of something called man" (*la disparition de quelque chose qui se serait appelé l'homme*), rather than the "advent of the overman" (*l'avènement du surhomme*), see Blanchot, *The Infinite Conversation*, 155; *L'Entretien infini*, 232.

82. Z, II (2006) "On the Famous Wise Men" 79; KSA, 4, 133: *das Fell des Raubthiers, das buntgefkeckte, and die Zotten des Forschenden, Suchenden, Erobernden*!
83. Z, II (in PN) "On the Famous Wise Men," 215; KSA 4, 133.
84. Ibid., 134.
85. Ibid.
86. Z, III (2006) "On the Vision and the Riddle," 124; KSA 4, 198.
87. Z, IV (2006) "The Magician," 204–5; KSA 4, 314–15.
88. For an analysis of "Ariadne's Complaint," see Del Caro, "Symbolizing Philosophy, vol. I, 82 f.
89. WP [1029]; KSA, 11, 33: *Ich habe die Erkenntniß vor so furchtbare Bilder gestellt, daß jeden "epikureische Vergnügen" dabei unmöglich ist. Nur die dionysische Lust reicht aus—ich habe das Tragische erst entdeckt. Bei den Griechen wurde es, dank ihrer moralistischen Oberflächlichkeit, mißverstanden. Auch Resignation ist nicht eine Lehre der Tragödie!—sondern ein Mißverständniß derselben ! Sehnsucht in's Nichts ist Verneinung der tragischen Weisheit, ihr Gegensatz!*
90. AC EH TI, on "The Birth of Tragedy," [3] 110; KSA 6, 312: *der erste tragische Philosoph.*
91. WLN, 79; KSA 12, 113: *Die Täuschung Apollos: die Ewigkeit der schönen Form; die aristokratische Gesetzgebung* "so soll es immer sein!" Dionysos: *Sinnlichkeit und Grausamkeit. Die Vergänglichkeit könnte ausgelegt werden als Genuß der zeugenden und zerstörenden Kraft, als beständige Schöpfung.*
92. Heidegger, *Nietzsche I* [En] 210; (Ger) *Nietzsche I*, 212.
93. Nietzsche refers to the relationship between the two artistic drives as the "capital question" in a preparatory note for *The Birth of Tragedy*: "Capital distinction between the Dionysian and the Apollonian art: each one with its own metaphysics. Capital question: what is the relationship of the two artistic drives to each other"— "*Hauptunterscheidung der dionysischen und der apollinischen Kunst: jede mit verschiedener Metaphysik. Hauptfrage: welches ist das Verhältnis beider Kunsttriebe zu einander?*—in *Gesammelte Werke*, edited by Max Oehler, vol. 3, 357; Albrecht, playing on words, identifies the *Hauptfrage* as the *Medusahaupt* (Medusa's head), thus pointing toward the danger of an aesthetic petrification, see his book *The Medusa Effect*, 51 ff.
94. BT (in BWN) "An Attempt at Self-Criticism" [4] 22; KSA 1, 17.
95. DB, 1 [9] 10; KSA 3, Morgenröte, 22: *die herkömmliche Art zu handeln und abzuschätzen.*
96. On "tragic cruelty" and "tragic knowledge" of the "terrifying, evil, questionable" (*Furchtbare, Böse, Fragwürdige*), see Nietzsche's notes from 1887/88, collected in WP [851, 852, and 853].
97. For an essential correlation between religious madness and cruelty, see Roberts, *Contesting Spirit*, 54.
98. AC EH TI, "Skirmishes of an Untimely Man," 24, 204; KSA 6, 127: *Was theilt der tragische Künstler von sich mit? Ist es nicht gerade der Zustand ohne Furcht vor dem Furchtbaren und Fragwürdigen, das er zeigt?*
99. GS 1 [26] 50; KSA 3, *Die fröhliche Wissenschaft* ("la gaya scienza"), 400.

100. GS 3 [125] 119–20; KSA 3, 481: *Wir haben ihn getödtet,—ihr und ich! Wir Alle sind seine Mörder!*

101. According to Nietzsche, all great prophets might have appeared as madmen to their contemporaries.

102. Heidegger, "Nietzsche's Word: 'God Is Dead,'" in *Off the Beaten Track*, 159–60 et passim; *Holzwege*, 212–13 et passim.

103. GS 3 [125] 119–20; KSA 3, *Die fröhliche Wissenschaft*, 481.

104. GS 3 [124] 119; KSA 3, *Die fröhliche Wissenschaft*, 480; Nostalgia for the firm land is an intuitive reaction to such experience of absolute freedom. But such *nost-algia* is a sickness, and it is a mortal sickness: for "there is no more 'land'" (*es gibt kein "Land" mehr*). The image might have been taken from Kant, who in his *Critique of Pure Reason*, after having analyzed and chartered the territory of pure understanding, presented it as an island of truth, surrounded by "a wide and stormy ocean, the native home of illusion" (*ein weit und stürmisch Ozean, der eigentlich Sitz des Scheins*)—Norman Kemp Smith's translation in Immanuel Kant, *Critique of Pure Reason*, 257: *Kritik der Reinen Vernunft* B 295, A 236; for Nietzsche, Kant's island of (the subject's) truth is itself an illusion; this comparison marks the radical character of Nietzsche's position; for a reading of Nietzsche in the perspective of (Kant's) critical project, see Deleuze, *Nietzsche et la philosophie*, 58f.

105. The "spirit of gravity" should not be confused with the "spirit of revenge" (*der Geist der Rache*), overcome by the doctrine of the eternal recurrence—see Heidegger, "Wer ist Nietzsches Zarathustra?" in his *Vorträge und Aufsätze*; "Who is Nietzsche's Zarathustra?" in his *Nietzsche* vol. II; cf. Müller-Lauter, "The Spirit of Revenge and the Eternal Recurrence," vol. III, 148–65.

106. Z, III (2006) "On the Spirit of Gravity," 153; KSA 4, 241.

107. HAH, I, "Man Alone with Himself," [531] 183; KSA 2, 326: *Wer davon lebt, einen Feind zu bekämpfen, hat ein Interesse daran, dass er am Leben bleibt.* ; cf. Z, I (2006) "On the Friend," 40.

108. Z, III (2006) "On the Spirit of Gravity,'" 156; KSA 4, 244.

109. Z, III (2006) "On the Three Metamorphoses," 16; KSA 4, 29.

110. Interpreters often point out Nietzsche's own experience of abandoning the victorious cause of Wagner's Bayreuth.

111. For a similar interpretation of the spirit of gravity, see for example H. L. Mencken, *The Philosophy of Friedrich Nietzsche*, 41–2; and in our time, Blondel, *Nietzsche: The Body and Culture*, p. 53; *Nietzsche: le corps et la culture*, p. 83; and especially, Rosen, for whom the spirit of gravity represents tradition—in his *Limits of Analysis*, 212; and finally Alejandro, *Nietzsche and the Drama of Historiography*, 68ff.

112. Z, III (2006) "On the Three Metamorphoses," 17; KSA 4, 30.

113. My translation from Deleuze, *Nietzsche*, 5: *le lion est présent dans le chameau, l'enfant est dans le lion; et dans l'enfant il y a l'issue tragique*.

114. Z, IV (2006) "The Leech," 202: *das Leben, das selber in's Leben schneidet*; KSA 4, 312.

115. GS, "Preface to the second edition," 4 (he has in mind the end of book IV of *The Gay Science*, from 1883).

116. GS, 4; cf. 3 [153] 132; KSA 3, 346 and 496.

117. For a similar play of "*para*" (*parergon*) in a deconstruction of traditional texts, see Derrida, *The Truth in Painting*, 15 ff.; *La vérité en peinture*, 19 ff.

118. GM (1989) I [11] 42; KSA 5, 276; see Nietzsche critique of journalism and of popularizing scholarship, such as Strauss's in his UM I.

119. GM (1989) 25; KSA 5, 258: *sogar der schlichten, herben, hässlichen, widrigen, unchristlichen, unmoralischen Warheit.*

120. AC EH TI, 121; KSA 6, 329–30: *nicht etwa mit der Grausamkeit jenes jungen Griechengottes, der das arme Eidechslein einfach anspiesste, aber immerhin doch mit etwas Spitzem, mit der Feder.*

121. Z, I (2006) "On Reading and Writing," 27; KSA 4, 48: *Schreibe mit Blut: und Du wirst erfahren, dass Blut Geist ist.*; see Babich, *Words in Blood, Like Flowers*, 19ff; cf. Derrida, *Spurs/Éperons*.

122. Z, II (2006) "On Priests," 71; KSA 4, 312: *Aber Blut ist der schlechteste Zeuge der Warheit; Blut vergiftet die reinste Lehre noch zu Wahn und Hass der Herzen.*

123. See Blanchot, *Infinite Conversation*, 153–4; "*La parole de fragment ignore les contradictions, même lorsqu'elle contredit.*"—*L'Entretien infini*, 230–1.

124. In KSA 5, *Zur Genealogie der Moral* 3 [12] 364: *eine Vergewaltigung und Grausamkeit an der Vernunft*); GM (1989) 3 [12] 118: "To renounce belief in one's ego, to deny one's own 'reality'—what a triumph! Not merely over the senses, over appearance, but a much higher kind of triumph, a violation and cruelty against *reason*."

125. Nietzsche, BKG, vol. III–1 286–8, a letter to Heinrich von Stein from December 1882: "*Man gewinnt etwas lieb: und kaum ist es Einem von Grund aus lieb geworden, so sagt der Tyrann in uns (den wir gar zu gerne 'unser höheres Selbst' nennen möchten): 'Gerade das gieb mir zum Opfer.' Und wir geben's auch—aber es ist Thierquälerei dabei und Verbranntwerden mit langsamen Feuer. Es sind fast lauter Probleme der Grausamkeit, die Sie behandeln: thut dies Ihnen wohl? Ich sage Ihnen aufrichtig, daß ich selber zuviel von dieser 'tragischen' Complexion im Leibe habe, um sie nicht oft zu verwünschen; meine Erlebnisse im Kleinen und Großen, nehmen immer den gleichen Verlauf. Da verlangt es mich am meisten nach einer Höhe, von wo aus gesehen das tragische Problem unter mir ist.—Ich möchte dem menschlichen Dasein etwas von seinem herzbrecherischen und grausamen Charakter nehmen. Doch, um hier fortfahren zu können, müßte ich Ihnen verrathen, was ich Niemandem noch verrathen habe—die Aufgabe, vor der ich stehe, die Aufgabe meines Lebens.*"
– see the comments of Higgins in her *Nietzsche's Zarathustra* 10–11, and of Allison, *Reading the New Nietzsche*, 74; cf. Schutte, *Beyond Nihilism*, 83.

Chapter 2

"Feeling of Thought"
Nietzsche's Critique of Terrible Abstractedness and Dostoevsky's Triumph in the Concrete

> Only literature dared to confront the nihilist cruelty of a real society.—
> André Glucksmann *Dostoïevski à Manhattan*[1]

One might consider, following Albert Camus, in a somewhat ahistorical way, Nietzsche's thought as being a preparation for Dostoevsky's achievement in literature ("triumph in the concrete"). Indeed, the "abstract powers of reason" have been humiliated in Nietzsche's thought more than in any other. The importance of this particular relationship between Nietzsche and Dostoevsky was already foreseen in 1903 in Leo Shestov's book *Dostoevsky and Nietzsche: The Philosophy of Tragedy*.[2] The problem of "nihilism today," and of cruelty, that is, the "untimely" problem of "our time" and of "our culture," warrants a further elaboration of this relationship. And, in the spirit of Shestov, this elaboration should not be forced into the dichotomy of a rational philosophical thought on the one hand, and "just literary fiction" (*ce n'est que la littérature*) on the other hand.[3] Neither Nietzsche's nor Dostoevsky's works can be simply subsumed under these categories, which are ultimately the "categories of reason" (*die Vernunftkategorien*). Nietzsche himself considered this view of philosophy to be responsible for the rise of cruelty and nihilism. Shestov's notion of the "philosophy of tragedy" has to be understood in the sense of questioning the notion of cruelty and of undermining the control of reason over affectivity.[4] Shestov draws a parallel between the persona of "Nietzsche" and Dostoevsky's characters based on thinking and writing as an experience of suffering and cruelty: "it is necessary for truth to cut us to the quick,"[5] he writes of Dostoevsky's art. One might think of Nietzsche's call for writing in blood in his *Thus Spoke Zarathustra*.[6] The two images—the true writing in blood and the surgical penetration of truth through the body—bring up the notion of cruelty as the principle of art in both Nietzsche and Dostoevsky.[7] The parallel of their views, of their prophetic force impose itself today even more than when Shestov was writing his pioneering work.[8]

NIETZSCHE AND DOSTOEVSKY

How liberating is Dostoevsky!—Friedrich Nietzsche[9]

In fact, Dostoevsky didn't know Nietzsche's work, and Nietzsche got to know Dostoevsky's only toward the end of his (conscious) life: "I did not even know the name of Dostoevsky just a few weeks ago, uncultured person that I am, not reading any journals," writes ironically Nietzsche to his friend Franz Overbeck on February 23, 1887.[10] He then expresses his extraordinary joy when reading *L'Esprit souterrain* (a French translation of the *Notes from Underground*). Nietzsche justifies this joy by the "instinct of kinship" with the just-discovered author. Indeed, how thrilled must have been Nietzsche when he had read that not only an excessive "consciousness is a sickness, a real thorough sickness,"[11] but that "any consciousness is a sickness"![12] Had he not diagnosed this very ailment in Western culture in his early books *The Birth of Tragedy* and *Untimely Meditations*? And didn't he finally express this diagnosis in a radical form in his *Gay Science*? Indeed, in the fifth book (from 1887) Nietzsche warns against the excess of consciousness: "In the end, the growing consciousness is a danger; and he who lives among the most conscious Europeans even knows it is a sickness."[13] Consciousness, like the unconscious "Screen memories" of Freud, should protect the minds from the cruelty of existence. Nietzsche found eventually a kindred spirit, someone who had seen the plight of modern Europeans. *Notes from Underground* began Dostoevsky's literary expression of this plight, and his struggle with the nihilism and cruelty of Western culture. For him, Saint Petersburg was the most extreme site of this plight (the "most abstract and intentional city in the world"), the site of the last man, the underground man, paralyzed, like Hamlet in Nietzsche's reading, by his acute consciousness, and yet, superior to those over-confident men of action, who are sooner or later fated to crash against the wall of natural laws and that of human culture.[14]

"Nihilism is ambiguous," it has always been, and yet one has always tried to deny this ambiguity and render the notion univocal and "univalent." Perhaps the essence of nihilism lies in this self-mystification. There are two aspects of nihilism that are usually evoked: The one "feeling of valuelessness" (*das Gefühl der Wertlosigkeit*) leading to an extreme passivity and the other an excessive belief in the "categories of reason" (*Vernunftkategorien*), and their domination over every domain of life. It is an open question whether these two aspects are essentially connected. The term "nihilism" was originally created in order to characterize a monism of one principle of all beings. It was Friedrich Heinrich Jacobi who reacted to the thought of unity of Johann Gottlieb Fichte, of an abstract, universal system stemming from one source; Jacobi called it "nihilism."[15] A monism of one principle (ἀρχή) begins with the prohibition of crossing the boundaries (*fines*) of definition. The univocity of rigorously defined terms would be an ideal of a "nihilist" point of view. And yet, nihilism is ambiguous, as Nietzsche famously stated.[16] In fact, this was "the only clear thing Nietzsche ever said about nihilism," according to Karen Carr. Otherwise, he characterized nihilism as "an historical process," "a psychological state," "a philosophical position," "a cultural condition," "a sign of weakness," "a sign of strength," "the danger of dangers," "a divine way of thinking."[17] Not all interpreters in the analytical tradition are as "clear" as Carr, but most of them would agree with her complaint that Nietzsche is "responsible for some of the conceptual confusions that attend most twentieth-century discussions of nihilism."[18] The principle of this condemnation, somewhat paradoxically, seems to be univocity—or at least, ordered polysemy—of concepts. A radical ambiguity characterizing nihilism would undermine this very principle (the Cartesian ideal of *notions claires et distinctes*); it would mark the limits of philosophical interpretation and point toward literature. The statement "feeling of thought" is also ambiguous. Belonging to different categories of the mind, intellect and feeling, these notions are hardly compatible.

PHILOSOPHY AND ART

A certain thought might prepare and free the way for literature, wrote Albert Camus. This would be a thought that would frustrate the unifying power of the abstract.[19] Indeed, "any thought that abandons unity glorifies diversity. And diversity is the home of art."[20] One should point out that this thought (feeling) is in direct opposition of Aristotle's *Poetics* and the neo-classicism with their insistence on unity(s). The recognition of the ambiguity of nihilism would be eventually not so much a matter of a rigorous argumentation as of *feeling*: what Dostoevsky's heroes call "feeling of thought" (*chuvstvo mysli*), and what Nietzsche specifies in respect to nihilism as "feeling of valuelessness." D. H. Lawrence wrote in his essay *The Novel and the Feelings* that "we have no language for the feelings," although "emotions are things we more or less recognize."[21] Literary mode is perhaps the only one to convey the feelings.[22] Nihilism, which is the object of this thought and of this feeling, is not just an example a theme for philosophical and literary consideration; it is the place of their modern confrontation, of the modern form of the "old quarrel" (*palaia diaphora*) between philosophy and poetry or art (*poiēsis*). To be sure, *nihil* or nothing is not a domain or territory like any other. *Nothing* marks an extreme boundary, the boundary of thought, the danger of extreme abstractedness (Dostoevsky's *otvlechennost'*).[23] To take the question of the *nothing* seriously is to take account of the ultimate boundaries of being, of the being of culture. The experience of boundaries is dangerous and deadly, and yet, vital.[24] Is culture able to come into contact with its ultimate boundaries before a crisis beyond repair?[25] The function of art and literature might be precisely to respond to this dilemma, to provide an experience with the extreme boundaries of culture, to traverse the danger of collapsing before the actual collapse.[26]

This is not an entirely new claim. Aristotle hinted at this function of literature when he wrote that, in contradistinction to "history" (a chronicle that merely registers what did happen), poetry considers what could have happened and what could happen: "It is not the poet's function to relate actual events (*ta genomena*), but the *kinds* of things that might occur (*hoia an genoito*) in terms of probability or necessity (*ta dunata kata to eikos ē to anankaion*)."[27] It is this common function of literature that performed Dostoevsky in his novel *Demons*, in showing what might occur, in displaying the ultimate consequences of political nihilism, although one could also point out that *Demons* contains elements of *ta genomena* in fictionalizing the Nechaev's case. Unfortunately, his "testimony," and his prophecy, has not been taken seriously enough, according to André Glucksmann and Albert Camus before him.[28] Glucksmann's book *Dostoïevski à Manhattan* was published in January 2002, just a few months after the events of September 11, 2001 in New York, and it is marked by the emotion following the events, and its judgment might be exaggerated in qualifying them as an extreme manifestation of nihilism; such a judgment, if narrowly understood, can be easily refuted by a political analysis *sensu stricto*.[29] But as a larger concept, it is certainly valid characterization of Western thought and its influence on Dostoevsky, as well as its reverberations in our modern world. If the perpetrators of the September 11 attacks cannot be simply qualified as mirror image of Russian terrorists from the nineteenth century, there is no doubt that we should consider this event as consequence of/reaction to nihilism in Western post-ideological society. As James Scanlan writes in the conclusion of his book *Dostoevsky the Thinker*: "Dostoevsky's profile as a philosophical thinker was shaped by his opposition to the ideas of the Russian Westernists, especially the more radical, 'Nihilistic' Westernists whose militant atheism and revolutionary socialism goaded him into formulating and defending his own fundamental believes."[30] Glucksmann's suggestion that the (historical) images of CNN should be "sub-titled" in Dostoevsky's language could only be justified if the latter was taken as a literary medium of an experience with nihilism in a broad sense.[31]

This is not the opinion of all Dostoevsky's readers. Dominique Janicaud discusses Dostoevsky's and Nietzsche's contribution to rethinking nihilism; and he refers to *Dostoïevski à Manhattan*. He rejects Glucksmann's interpretation of a prophetic and philosophical Dostoevsky.[32] Not having been a true historian (a depiction of the "true Nechaev" was not his interest in the *Demons*), Dostoevsky was not a philosopher either: "in vain one would look for a rigorous analysis of nihilism in his book; there is neither definition nor ideological position, nor argumentation (nor counter-argumentation), nor resorting to a metaphysical tradition (other than the religious horizon of Evil)."[33] For Janicaud, Dostoevsky belongs to the domain of myth even if, in a modern fashion, he makes his characters move in an atmosphere of "*intellectuality* with its procession of ratiocinations and justifications for the purpose in hand."[34] To be sure, Dostoevsky is a writer of genius; Janicaud calls him "*génial*" a little bit like the philosopher Socrates called his contemporary poets "divine" (*theoi*) only in order to refuse their testimony of the truth of being.[35] Dostoevsky's perspective, according to Janicaud, is limited by his religious views, by his supposed Manichaeism of good and evil (*l'empire du Mal d'un côté, l'empire du divin de l'autre*).[36] The evident fact that Slavophile Dostoevsky cannot be considered to be fully Orthodox doesn't make him necessarily a Manichean. Glucksmann is wrong, in Janicaud's view, to take Dostoevsky seriously as a philosopher and to use his insight in the interpretation of the events of September 11, 2001, and of other contemporary catastrophes, of other "manifestations of nihilism." He is wrong to consider Nietzsche and Dostoevsky on the same level. Indeed Nietzsche, is "ahead of" Dostoevsky in his analysis of nihilism, and precisely as a philosopher concerned with argumentation.[37] Albert Camus had already remarked long time before this debate that if Dostoevsky limited himself to the rigorous, moral, and metaphysical argumentation, he would have been a philosopher; instead, "he illustrates the consequences that such intellectual pastimes may have in a man's life, and in this regard he is an artist."[38]

In what follows, I shall consider nihilism as the place of the modern version of the "old quarrel" between philosophy and literature, in the framework of which Janicaud's argumentation, and that of so many contemporary philosophers and literary critics, seems to be confined. I shall claim that neither Nietzsche nor Dostoevsky fit neatly into the traditionally established academic divisions. The problematic of nihilism transcends the traditionally circumscribed fields, such as philosophy, psychology, literature, literary studies, and criticism. Bessa Myftiu puts it well: "Nietzsche and Dostoevsky. Incompatible, perhaps, at the first glance. Similar at the second. Independently of the fact that one is considered a philosopher and the second a writer, I will qualify Nietzsche as a philosopher writing poetry and Dostoevsky as a novelist writing philosophy. This works also the other way around. Philosophy rejoins art. Art rejoins philosophy."[39]

ART AS A DISTINCTIVE COUNTERMOVEMENT TO NIHILISM

Our religion, morality, and philosophy are decadence-forms of man. The *countermovement: art.*—Nietzsche, *Will to Power*[40]

Philosophy, and the sciences, relying on rational arguments, on univocally defined concepts and categories, separate or supposedly separate themselves from the "fiction" of literature, and thus, deprive themselves of the singular experience of potentiality, or in this case rather impotence. In Nietzsche's view, the roots of nihilism reside in the excessive "trust in the categories of reason" (*der Glaube an die Vernunftkategorien*), and in their eventual collapse.[41] Literature, in Dostoevsky and in Turgenev before him, resists such a reduction, not only because of the art of the authors, but also because of the pressure of the "things themselves" (*auta ta pragmata*),[42] as Aristotle would say, which in the case of nihilism would rather mean "no-things."

If Turgenev's Bazarov was the most famous nihilist character in literature, and Nietzsche the most "accomplished" nihilist in philosophy, Nechaev was probably the most discussed nihilist in political history.[43] To be sure, he became also a literary character, under the name of Pyotr Verkhovensky in Dostoevsky's novel *Demons* (1871/2), and under his own name in Coetzee's novel *The Master of Petersburg* (1994).[44] The "historical" Sergey Nechaev, a disciple and friend of Mikhail Bakunin, an author (perhaps a co-author with Bakunin) of the infamous *Catechism of a Revolutionary* (1869; not to be confused with Bakunin's *Revolutionary Catechism*, 1866),[45] together with his comrades from "*People's Vengeance*" (*Narodnaia rasprava*), murdered in Moscow in 1869 a student Ivan Ivanov, suspected of betrayal. This event confirmed and largely publicized the negative valuation of the notion and word "nihilism." It also incited Dostoevsky to write his novel: "Details from the Nechaev affair remain prominent in the text of *Demons*, as well. Apart from details of the real-life murder itself, reflected in the murder of Shatov, the novel retains recognizable vestiges of both Sergei Nechaev and his accomplices, as well as their organizational principles."[46] But if the affair Ivanov/Nechaev directly triggered the writing of *Demons*, the novel was not the first confrontation of Dostoevsky with nihilism. Even though he did not use the word either in his *Notes from a Dead House* or in *Notes from Underground*, Dostoevsky did reflect in these works on some aspects of his own and his contemporaries' experience that were later summed up in the notion of nihilism. Most of the commentators place the *Notes* at the origin of all later reflection and creation of Dostoevsky[47]—at the origin of (his) truth, which, according to Lev Shestov had to lead "through deportation, the dungeon, and the underground."[48]

HISTORICAL AND LITERARY TRUTH

"There is no other way to truth than through deportation, the dungeon, and the underground," Leo Shestov wrote in 1903.[49] In both *Notes from a Dead House* and *Notes from Underground*, fiction conveys the historical truth, testifies to the crisis of contemporary society. In both works, death is associated with the general, abstract view of the world, and is opposed to the singular experience of life. This is especially true of the *Notes from Underground*, where the "truth" of "two times two is four is no longer life, . . . but the beginning of death."[50] Abstract reasoning is to be sure a good thing, but it is only a fraction, perhaps only "twentieth part" of human life.[51] The rest might be "a bit of trash," but it is still life Human nature as a whole might be epistemologically unreliable—might be consciously or unconsciously lying—but this doesn't diminish its vitality: "though it lies, still it lives" (*i khot' vryot, da zhivyot*).[52] The underground man is a "spiteful" man: a nihilist, a passive nihilist marked by impotence, unable to become anything, unable even to become positively evil. To become evil would require some passion, which this nihilist lacks. To be sure, a nihilist can theoretically accept or reject the authority of calculative reason, but he is unable to affirm life in practice, that is to live, at least not in the sense of a "real living life" (*nastoiashchej zhivoj zhizni*). And yet this spite, this gratuitous *zlost'* (evil, anger) could perhaps lead to an overcoming of passivity, to the pessimism of strength. The underground man claims to have conducted such dangerous experience: "I have merely carried to an extreme in my life what you have not dared to carry even halfway," he tells his readers, and he makes this final diagnosis of his contemporaries: "you've taken your cowardice for good sense, and found comfort in thus deceiving yourselves." Again, the underground man's "nihilism," because of his self-awareness, gives some hopes of overcoming; he eventually comes out more "living" than his readers.[53] To be sure, this challenge to his contemporaries is mitigated by the fictional editor of the *Notes*, who represents the common opinion (*doxa*). He distances himself from the underground nihilist by calling him a "paradoxalist."[54]

Notes from a Dead House, published two years earlier, are less insistent on the opposition between general speculation and the singular experience of life, but the opposition is already there. The hero/narrator tries to categorize his fellow prisoners, but eventually has to acknowledge the failure of this theoretical enterprise: "Reality is infinitely diverse compared to all, even the most clever, conclusions of abstract thought."[55] The singular life of the prisoners resists classification. Again, only art and literature would be able to do justice to such variation in life, to allow a consideration of infinite possibility, which in *Notes from a Dead House* includes both life and death, and the gradation between them; for example, the cruel punishment, whipping, which often leads to death. Indeed, the "dead house" is not simply dead (*mertvyj*) but "living dead" (*zazhivo mertvyj dom*, "alive dead house," "the house of the living dead").[56] Russian *zazhivo* is an adverb modifying the adjective *mertvyj* or dead, and thus, rather than denoting the state of being dead, it points out its dynamic, "lively" character. In fact, the very next word following the expression "dead house" and in an apposition to it, is life (*zhizn'*): this is the experience the author of the *Notes* is describing. Again, the word "nihilism" is not used in these *Notes*, but the extreme situation of the proximity of life and death renders particularly acute the importance of the will to live (and thus a negation of a passive nihilism) for the survival in the particular circumstances of the prison fortress.

IDEAS IN *DEMONS*

> It has been said of Dostoevsky that he "feels" or "sees ideas,"—
> Glucksmann, *Dostïevski à Manhattan*[57]

The question of nihilism in *Demons*, the novel that would justify Glucksmann's pronouncement of a prophetic Dostoevsky, is inscribed in the tension of life and death. Life and death seem inseparable in the experience of Kirillov, one of the "nihilists" in *Demons*. To be sure, Kirillov himself wants to separate the two and to deny death altogether. When Stavrogin, his friend, points out the apparent incompatibility of Kirillov's passion for life and his decision to commit suicide, he answers impatiently (in his particular, choppy way): "So what? Why together? Life's separate, and that's separate. Life is, and death is not at all."[58] Kirillov's denial of death in favor of "earthly eternity," the eternity of particularly intense moments, is as little understood as will later Nietzsche's idea of eternal recurrence. Both are certainly the "highest formulas of affirmation," but they don't seem to function on a logical level. In any case, no one in Dostoevsky's novel understands/accepts Kirillov's claim to life and happiness through death. Theoretically, his paradox appears as a logical fallacy or as a "drawing-room joke," comparable to the one pointed to him by Stepan Vierkhovensky: "you want to build our bridge, and at the same time you declare yourself for the principle of universal destruction. They'll never let you build our bridge!"[59] This objection is met with Kirillov's childlike laughter that shows his candidness in the face of, and at the same time the rejection of, logical reasoning; his ideas, his thoughts are the matter of feeling rather than of an impassive speculation.[60]

Apparently a similar phenomenon of strictly logical inferences resulting in paradoxical consequences is presented in the theory of Shigalyov, one of the revolutionaries, whose speech is also met with the bemused reaction of the more down-to-earth audience. Starting with the principle of "unlimited freedom," through a rigorous reasoning, Shigalyov arrives at the state of "unlimited despotism."[61] He is aware of the fact that his conclusions contradict the original idea, but he assures that there is no other solution to this general social problem. One would be tempted to compare the two cases, Kirillov's and Shigaylov's, the "entanglement" in an idea.[62] In fact, such comparison would only reveal their radical difference. To be sure, both characters personify the ambiguity of nihilism. But in Shigalyov's case the ambiguity is played out on the theoretical level. It causes an annoyance for analytical minds; it is a logical problem or, in Kirillov's serious view, a "drawing-room joke."[63] The dismissal of Shigalyov's conundrum as a serious problem in *Demons* is possible because he is not a full-blown character, but only a somewhat comic support of an idea and of logical contradiction. In the character of Kirillov, on the other hand, we have it all; a full name with a patronymic: Alexei Nilych, his physical characterization, and a glimpse into his soul, or his thoughts, which he would feel rather than simply think. We have also his unmistakable, idiosyncratic way of talking, which makes sometimes doubt he is a native Russian; in fact, he ends up by presenting himself in his suicide note as both Russian noble and a "citizen of the civilized world" (*citoyen du monde civilisé*).[64] And it is true that it is the entire world that Kirillov wants to save through his act of "philosophical (pedagogical) suicide."[65] It will prove (or rather show) that man is free and god-like, "man-god" (*chelovekobog*), rather than, like Christ, "God-man" (*bogochelovek*).[66] For Kirillov, who already knows (feels) this "human divinity," life in all its most simple manifestations—a moldy yellow leaf, a spider crawling on the wall—is not only compatible with death, but requires it for its own unconditional affirmation. Suicide, rather than simple killing of someone else, is a harmonious affirmation of one's self-will (*svoevolie*).[67] The actual cruel scene of Kirillov's suicide is far from harmonious though. The ambiguity of nihilism, of which Kirillov's reasoning is one of the exhibitions, loses its character of a logical puzzle and becomes serious, even tragic.

WORDS AND DEEDS

> All my life I did not want it to be merely words.—Kirillov, in Dostoevsky's Demons[68]

Camus suggests the tragic interpretation of *Demons* when in his essay *The Myth of Sisyphus*, he discusses Kirillov's suicide with references to Aeschylus' *Prometheus Bound* and *Agamemnon*.[69] Camus calls it *une indicible aventure spirituelle*.[70] Kirillov is to bring humanity freedom and life without fear of death. Like the chorus from *Agamemnon*, he affirms repeatedly, "everything is good" (*vsyo kharasho*).[71] As Ray Davison pointed out: "Camus links Kirilov's thought to the main thesis of *Le Mythe de Sisyphe*, that the absurd can bring passionate happiness to mankind."[72] Like in the case of Sisyphus, according to Camus, one must imagine Kirillov happy. He identifies his tragic fate when he says that like Stavrogin he had been devoured by an idea.[73] Universal destruction and his own annihilation seem paradoxically a condition *sine qua non* of Kirillov's affirmation of life and his happiness. Considered from a theoretical point of view, they seem completely separate, and mutually dependent only because of an entanglement in an idea. But one can hardly say, with Cicovacki, that Kirillov "lives in the clouds of ideas," whereas "Stavrogin needs to be in touch with the real world."[74] One might even say the opposite, especially when one thinks of the Russian word for "reality," *dejstvitel'nost'*, closely related to the adjective *dejstvitel'nyj*, eventually originating from the verb *dejstvovat'* (Greek *ergein*, Latin *agere*) or to act, that is modern *dejstvie* or action, activity, *ergon*.[75] "Reality" in Russian would thus be rather *pragma* than *res*, a human, "practical" (in Aristotelian, moral sense) action, requiring an emotional engagement. Contrary to Stavrogin—who mostly refrains from action: from responding to Shatov's insult, from shooting Gaganov in the duel, from saving the young girl, from preventing the murder of Maria Timofeevna and her brother and expresses his cruelty in this way—Kirillov engages in reality, he positively acts, and acts without mediation of an idea: he defends Maria Timofeevna, tries to prevent the duel, helps Shatov after the return of his pregnant wife, and so forth. Responding to Verkhovensky's dismissal of moral judgment as "only words," Kirillov says angrily: "All my life I did not want it to be only words. This is why I lived, because I kept not wanting it. And now, too, every day I want it not to be words."[76] It is this direct engagement with life that renders his fate, his suicide and his association with Pyotr Verkhovensky tragic; there is no trace of "parody" in his final act.[77] One might think that if we had the same intimate view of Shigalyov, he might also appear as a tragic, rather than comic, character. Only on a superficial level can nihilist idea appear as attractive or ridiculous. The character of Verchovensky (the image of Nechaev) is entirely determined by an abstract idea.

S. N. Bulgakov attributes Verkhoviensky's cruelty, which he displays at each step of the way, to the cruelty of his nihilistic idea: "Verkhovensky rests perfectly consequent and sincere in his mendacity, in his adventurism, and in his courage—which one should not deny—he serves his idea. And if he is horrifying and even loathsome it is because his idea is horrific."[78] It becomes tragic when confronted with real-life emotional experience. Virghinsky's and Lyamshin's (the revolutionaries and assassins of Szatov) reaction illustrate this incompatibility between an idea (the idea of revolution), a cruel idea and life. When confronted with blood, the idea loses its theoretical purity, becomes tainted with feeling, cruel: "it's not it" (*eto ne to*), keeps repeating obsessively Virghinsky after the murder.[79]

But is not Shigalyov's abstract reasoning raised to the tragic level after all, namely, in the character of Pyotr Stepanovich Verkhovensky? He is Shigalyovist as well; "I'm for Shigalyovism," he says, presenting his utopian vision of a police state, with the "Pope on top."[80] However, Pyotr Verkhovensky is willing to drop both the Pope and Shigalyovism; what interests him is "actuality" (*zloba dnia*, literally the evil of the day), "dirty work" (*chiornaia rabota*). When he and Kirillov seem finally to agree on a certain "moral nihilism" ("all men are scoundrels," says Kirillov; "everyone's the same," agrees Verkhovensky, "no one's better or worse"), this nihilist view is another reason for Kirillov to kill himself, and for Verkhovensky, only a justification for continuing his dirty work.[81] He is certainly not "eaten by an idea"; he is just willing to use all "little ideas" (*idejki*), and especially the idea of destruction (*razrushenie*), the most captivating.[82] Like Plato's philosopher-king, he will have recourse to "noble lies" (*gennaya pseudē*), although he cannot care less for the nobility part. Shigalyovism is for him just one of those little ideas. Perhaps he is right when he repeatedly calls himself *mashennik* or crook, rather than socialist.[83] He is ready to discard the idea of "philanthropy" or Shigalyovism for at least two generations in favor of an "unheard-of depravity" that will turn men into cowards and cruel egoists. In fact, Verkhovensky's relation to little ideas (all of them are "little" for him) reveals, by contrast, Kirillov's tragedy of being devoured by an idea, of feeling his thoughts in the flesh.

But what about Vierkhovensky's "love" for Stavrogin? Is not Stavrogin the corner stone of his utopian vision? Is he not devoured by his passion for an idea (of beauty)? He appeals to Stavrogin as a leader and a sun, as a "terrible aristocrat" needed in order to captivate the democrats. Without Stavrogin, Verkhovensky would be "a fly, an idea in a bottle, Columbus without America."[84] But the America he needs is in fact a mythical entity, a legend, and he is able to produce legends himself. Eventually, Verkhovensky discusses his politics in aesthetic terms: "I am a nihilist, but I love beauty," he says, and asks: "Do nihilists not love beauty?" In his excitement, Pyotr Verkhovensky considers Stavrogin an incarnation of beauty, and he calls him an "idol" (*idol*). If one pronounces this last word in Plato's Greek, *eidolon*, and one hears behind it "little idea" (*idejka*) or simulacrum (*phantasma*), it can ultimately be discarded like all other little ideas, all simulacra, as for example Shigalyovism. Thus, Verkhovensky doesn't seem overly disturbed by Stavrogin's disappearance; after all, it is the myth that is important, and he can produce and control it. As in all other cases, his "love" for Stavrogin does not prevent him from proceeding lucidly and efficaciously.

Pyotr Verkhovensky is not a simple caricature of Sergey Nechaev, of a nihilist in the most common sense of the word; in Dostoevsky's novel he also functions as the instigator, but also the revealer for all other representatives of nihilism. Toward the end of his breathtaking exchange with Stavrogin, his idol, for example, he asks with the last hope: "Stavrogin, is America ours?" And when Stavrogin answers with a question, which might encapsulate the attitude of passive nihilism, "what for?" (*zachem*?; cf. Nietzsche's *das Warum?*), Verkhovensky expresses his disappointment: "No desire, I just knew it!" But he still cannot believe in Stavrogin's apathy: "You are lying, you rotten, lascivious, pretentious little squire, I don't believe you, you've got a wolf's appetite!"[85] The truth is, however, that Stavrogin is not lying; he doesn't have a wolf's appetite at all. In fact, all his endeavors tend to stimulate such an appetite, a desire to act.

Liza Knapp reduces the problem of passive nihilism to the predominance among most intellectuals in the mid-nineteenth century Russia, of a materialist view of the world, which she calls, after Dostoevsky's characters (she mentions Liputin (theoretic Proudonist) from *Demons* and the husband in *The Meek One*), "inertia."[86] Contrary to Shestov's questioning mode ("Where did this inertia come from, this boundless power of death over life?"),[87] Knapp attributes this phenomenon unambiguously to the positivist and scientist development in the Russian culture of this time.[88] It is Shatov who best expresses the opinion of Dostoevsky in this case of passive nihilism. After having questioned the ability of the intelligentsia educated in Western materialist view of sciences to believe in God (especially "in the mystery of the Word becoming flesh"), Shatov denies as well the ability of the present generation to unite with the people. Such faith and such reunion would require a distance from the institution of serfdom and at the same time the liberation from Western-European influences.[89]

KIRILLOV'S CONONDRUM

Dying is more honorable than killing.—Seneca, *Epistulae Morales*[90]

But is not Shatov eventually Stavrogin's disciple? He explicitly calls him his teacher: "There wasn't any 'our' conversation: there was a teacher uttering immense words, and there was a disciple who rose from the dead. I am that disciple and you are the teacher."[91] And Stavrogin is also a source of inspiration for Kirillov, and even in a sense for Pyotr Verkhovensky. He himself wonders at this exceptional role attributed to him: "why is it that everyone is foisting some banner on me?"[92] Why indeed believe in someone who is unable to believe in oneself? Stavrogin's charisma relies on his infinite potentiality, a potentiality never realized. It is perhaps Kirillov who best diagnoses the ultimate problem of nihilism in Stavrogin, as well as the general problem of passive and active nihilism, and of a possible transition from the one to the other.[93] After suggesting that Stavrogin was "*also* devoured by an idea," Kirillov pronounces an enigmatic phrase (immediately dismissed as "silly" by Pyotr Vierkhovensky): "If Stavrogin believes, he does not believe that he believes. If he does not believe, he does not believe that he does not believe."[94] This, Pevear and Volokhonsky's, translation is fairly literal.[95] So is Nietzsche's German translation: "*wenn er glaubt, glaubt er nicht, daß er glaubt. Wenn er nicht glaubt, glaubt er nicht daß er nicht glaubt*";[96] and also Camus' French translation: "*Si Stavroguine croit, il ne croit pas qu'il croie. S'il ne croit pas, il ne croit pas qu'il ne croie pas.*"[97]

I quoted these translations not only to show Nietzsche's and Camus' interest in this encapsulation of the most striking aspect of nihilism, but also in order to suggest the need for literality here (and in other cases of apparently enigmatic formulas). Not all translations respect it; Justin O'Brien's translation of Kirillov's judgment in Camus' inscription to the chapter "The Absurd Man" of his *Myth of Sisyphus* doesn't convey the serious play of Dostoevsky, and then, of Nietzsche and of Camus himself: "If Stavrogin believes, he does not think he believes. If he does not believe, he does not think he does not believe."[98] The distinction between thinking and believing in O'Brien's translation, in other words, the reduction of the double meaning of *verit'*, *glauben*, *croire*, and *believe*, suggests a distinction between two faculties, one intellectual, cognitive (thinking), the other passionate (feeling, belief). To be sure, in Stavrogin's case, one might say that the latter is controlled and reduced by the former, as suggests Stavrogin's letter to Darya Pavlovna: "I can never lose my mind or reason, nor can I ever believe an idea to the same degree as he [Kirillov] did. I cannot even entertain an idea to the same degree. I could never, never shoot myself."[99] In the conclusion of the book the narrator reports a similar judgment of the town people concerning Pyotr Verkhovensky. He was marked by "a total ignorance of reality" and by "a terrible abstractedness."[100] The fact that Stavrogin commits suicide after all, and precisely by hanging himself (as one of his victims, Matryosha, did), shows that such reduction, at least in some cases, is impossible. Stavrogin seems to have foreseen it himself in his predicament when he first talked about his feeling of the thought of suicide.[101] The case of Stavrogin suggests an association of abstractedness with cruelty. One may adduce as a proof of the general attitude of Dostoevsky a quote from *Notes from Underground,* where the hero confesses: "although I did this cruelty [cruelty toward Liza] on purpose, it came not from my heart, but from my stupid head." "This cruelty was so affected, so much from the head, so purposely contrived, so *bookish* that I myself could not bear it even for a minute."[102] Because "reasoning explains nothing, and consequently there is no point in reasoning."[103]

Thus, one can hardly reduce Kirillov's statement to a simple intellectual hesitation as to the state of belief or its lack. The doubling of the key verb indicates a basic existential attitude: will to believe. Man would believe in nothing rather than not believe, one might paraphrase Nietzsche's dictum.[104] Stavrogin seems to be aware of this need to believe, but he is unable to believe even in nothing.[105] This is exactly what Kirilov's sentence is saying, and Stavrogin's letter confirms it: "what poured out of me was only negation, with no magnanimity and no force. Or not even negation." He envies the ordinary nihilists (the negators) their hopes. Contrary to "magnanimous Kirillov," Stavrogin can "endure" any idea, even the negation of all ideas, without being touched by it, without "feeling" it, without believing in it. Just as Nietzsche's "will to will," will to believe, is concomitant with life,[106] or as the poet Vyacheslav Ivanov wrote, on "being" in Dostoevsky: "belief and unbelief are neither two different explanations of the world, nor two different guidance in life, but two essentially different kinds of being."[107] It is not surprising that the lack of belief in this sense has to end in death.[108]

The chapter "At Tikhon" (also referred to as "Stavrogin's Confession")—a chapter that has been suppressed by the censorship of 1872, but is now restored by some editors (toward the end of Part II of the *Demons*) or at least printed as an appendix—supports this view of Stavrogin, and of Dostoevsky, by Tikhon's dramatic reading (on Stavrogin's request) of the Apocalypse Revelation 3:14–22, focusing on the following passage: "I know thy works, that thou art neither cold nor hot: I would thou wert cold or hot. So then because thou art lukewarm, and neither cold nor hot, I will spue thee out of my mouth." In terms that recall the original meaning of nihilism in Anacharsis Cloots, Tikhon points out the extreme danger of "worldly indifference," and compares it with atheism: "a complete atheist stands on the next-to-last upper step to the most complete faith, while the indifferent one has no faith, apart from a bad fear."[109] The development of the conversation forces Stavrogin to identify with the worldly indifference or in other words passive nihilism. Far from limiting this passive nihilism to an exceptional case such as Stavrogin's, Dostoevsky in his *Diary of a Writer* from 1876 diagnoses with a strange "universal indifference" (*indifferentizm*) the whole Russian society of his time; this nihilism of indifference veils the truth of life.[110]

In the case of Stavrogin, the indifference ends with death. To be sure, Kirillov dies too, but just before his suicide he asserts, repeatedly, his will to "believe in unbelief" as the only way to proclaim his self-will (*svoevole*): "it is my duty to believe that I do not believe."[111] This is the most dramatic confirmation of the ambiguity of nihilism, here in relation to death. Death can mean a negation or an affirmation of life. In Stavrogin's case, it is the admission of utter impotence, in Kirillov's case, a supreme affirmation of the self-will, of the will to will.[112] These two aspects of nihilism—in Nietzsche's words "indifference" (*adiaphora*)[113] and "*faith in unbelief* to the point of martyrdom"—have certainly marked the history of the two centuries of nihilism, which Nietzsche foretold, and which still determine our history/destiny (*Geschichte*). They constitute the ultimate sense of the ambiguity of nihilism (*indifferentizm* and *svoevole* in Dostoevsky). We know it perhaps, but we need to realize that it is also the question of feeling, the feeling of thought. Glucksmann's call for rereading Dostoevsky, and for literary questioning in general, has to be understood in the sense of this need.

NOTES

1. (my translation) 266: *Seule la littérature se permit d'affronter la cruauté nihiliste d'une société réelle.*

2. George Steiner, in his Postface to the French edition of 2008, considers tracing of the parallel between the two thinkers the main insight of the book—Chestov, *La philosophie de la tragédie*, 279f.

3. Ibid., 262; *Достоевский и Ницше (философия трагедии)*, 208.

4. See some recent rereading of Shestov's work on Nietzsche and Dostoevski in "Léon Chestov/Jean-Luc Nancy," in *Europe. Revue Littéraire Mensuelle*.

5. Shestov, *Dostoevsky, Tolstoy and Nietzsche*, XXV, 285 (literally "the truths have to penetrate our body as knives," "*наконец, нужно, чтобы истины врезались в тело словно ножом*," cf. *La philosophie de la tragédie*, 229f; Shestov presents the same view of the function of Dostoevsky's art as his contemporary Mikhailovsky: a cruel exacerbation of suffering; see Mikhailovsky, *Dostoevsky. A Cruel Talent*, 29.

6. Z, "On Reading and Writing," (2006), 27: "Write with blood, and you will experience that blood is spirit." KSA, vol. 4, "Vom Lesen und Schreiben," 48.

7. See Mikhailovsky, *Dostoevsky: A Cruel Talent*, 29.

8. See the most recent rereading of Shestov's work on Nietzsche and Dostoevsky in *Europe. Revue Littéraire Mensuelle*.

9. (my translation); *Nachlaß. 1887–1889* KSA 13, 14[47] 241: *Wie erlösend ist Dostoiewsky!*

10. In BKG vol. III, 5, 27–8: *Von Dostoiewsky wußte ich vor wenigen Wochen auch selbst den Namen nicht—ich ungebildeter Mensch, der keine "Journale" liest! Ein zufälliger Griff in einem Buchladen brachte mir das eben ins Französische übersetzte Werk L'Esprit souterrain unter die Augen . . . Der Instinkt der Verwandtschaft (oder wie soll ich's nennen?) sprach sofort, meine Freude war außerordentlich: ich*

muß bis zu meinem Bekanntwerden mit Stendhals "Rouge et noir" zurückgehen, um einer gleichen Freude mich zu erinnern; cf. Kaufmann, *Nietzsche: Philosopher, Psychologist, Antichrist*, 318.

11. Dostoevsky, NU, 6; ЗП vol. 2, 612: *slishkom soznavat'—eto bolezn', nastoiashchaia, polnaia bolezn'*.

12. Dostoevsky, NU 6; ЗП, vol. 2, 612: *vsiakoe soznanie bolezn'*.

13. GS [354], 214; "Die fröhliche Wissenschaft" KSA 3 [354], 593.

14. Dostoevsky, NU, II, : ЗП, vol. 2, 613: *samyj otvlechennyj i umyshlennyj gorod na vsem zemnom share*.

15. Jacobi, "Letter to Fichte" from 3 March 1799, in *The Main Philosophical Writings*, 519; *Jacobi an Fichte*, in *Werke*, 39; cf. *Nihilismus*, ed. Dieter Arendt, 107.

16. Nietzsche wrote it in his posthumously published notes from 1888: "Nihilismus. Er ist *zweideutig*," KSA 12, 9[35] 350f.; Nietzsche, WLN, 146; cf. Löwith, *Von Hegel zu Nietzsche*, 208.

17. Carr, *The Banalization of Nihilism*, 27.

18. Ibid., 151, n. 2; cf. Solomon, "Nietzsche, Nihilism, and Morality," in *Nietzsche: A Collection of Critical Essays*.

19. "The essential is that the novelists should triumph in the concrete and that this constitute their nobility. This wholly carnal triumph has been prepared for them by a thought in which abstract powers have been humiliated"—Camus, *The Myth of Sisyphus*, 116; *Le myth de Sisyphe*, 155; see Deleuze's discussion of the thought that in Nietzsche's thought "ceases to be a *ratio*," in *Nietzsche and Philosophy*, 101; *Nietzsche et la philosophie*, 116: *la pensée cesse d'être une* ratio.

20. Camus, *The Myth of Sisyphus*, 116; *Le myth de Sisyphe*, 155: "*Toute pensée qui renounce à l'unité exalte la diversité. Et la diversité est le lieu de l'art.*"

21. Lawrence, "The Novel and the Feelings," 756–7.

22. Dostoevsky, D, 236; Б, 204; Nietzsche, WLN, 11[99]1: 219; KSA 13, 11[99]1, 48; The transliteration in the text follows the ICAO (International Civil Aviation Organization) system from 2013 (order No. 320), published in, "*Machine Readable Travel Documents,*" Part 1, Volume 1, ICAO. 2006.IV-50–IV-52, updated November 29, 2013, with the addition of "j" to mark й (as distinct from и), and an apostrophe (') to mark the soft sign (softening the preceding consonant) "ь."

23. See Heidegger on *nihil* in the lecture-course "Der europäische Nihilismus," in his *Nietzsche* [Ger] II Band, 42: *das Nichts aus der Verneinung, dem Neinsagen, ist ein bloßes Denkgebilde, das Abstrakteste des Abstrakten*; English: "European Nihilism," in *Nietzsche*, IV [Eng] 21: "The nothing of negation or no-saying is a mere mental image, the most abstract of abstractions."

24. Bakhtin, "The Problem of Content, Material, and Form in Verbal Act (1924)," 274: "Every cultural act lives essentially on the boundaries, and it derives its seriousness and significance from this fact. Separated by abstraction from these boundaries, it loses the ground of its being and becomes vacuous, arrogant; it degenerates and dies."—Михаил М. Бахтин, *Вопросы Литературы и Эстетики*, 25.

25. Glucksmann poses the question in terms of a conflict of "nihilism against civilization," in *Dostoïevski à Manhattan*, 109, and in terms of a dramatic alternative "nihilism or civilization" in his *Ouest contre Ouest*, 36.

26. On the etymology of "experience" and its importance for defining poetry and literature, see Lacoue-Labarthe, *Poetry as Experience*, 18 et passim; *La poésie comme expérience*, 30.

27. "οὐ τὸ τὰ γενόμενα λέγειν, τοῦτο ποιητοῦ ἔργον ἐστίν, ἀλλ᾽ οἷα ἂν γένοιτο καὶ τὰ δυνατὰ κατὰ τὸ εἰκὸς ἢ τὸ ἀναγκαῖον"—Aristotle, *Poetics*, 1450a36–9; the optative with ἂν (ἂν γένοιτο) expresses potentiality, a future possibility; see Smyth, *Greek Grammar*, 407f.

28. As Natov writes in her article "Albert Camus' Attitude toward Dostoevsky": "Camus considered this novel a prophetic book not only because it prefigured modern nihilism and the rejection of all accepted values, but also because the problem of conflicts of Dostoevsky's protagonists are the focus of modern man," 456.

29. See Golsan, "Preliminary Reflections on Anti-antiaméricanisme: André Glucksmann et compagnie," 391–404 and Sartarelli, "Where Did Our Love Go," 30; Neyrat, *Le Terrorisme, un concept piégé*, 69ff; cf., on the other hand, Nishimura, "E. H. Carr, Dostoevsky, and the Problem of Irrationality in Modern Europe," 45–64.

30. Scanlan, *Dostoevsky the Thinker*, 231.

31. Glucksmann, *Dostoïevski à Manhattan*, 24: *Dostoïevski et ses "Démons" eussent judicieusement sous-titré les images livrées en boucle sur CNN*.

32. Cf. Valentino's questioning of a prophetic Dostoevsky on purely, literary/rhetorical grounds in his "The Word Made Flesh in Dostoevskii's *Possessed*," 49.

33. Janicaud, "La postérité des *Possédés*," 124.

34. Ibid., 125.

35. See e.g., Plato, *Ion*, 534d.

36. Janicaud, "La postérité des *Possédés*," 129.

37. Ibid., 127.

38. Camus, *The myth of Sisyphus*, 104; *Le mythe de Sisyphe*, 140: *il illustre les conséquences que ces jeux de l'esprit peuvent avoir dans une vie d'homme et c'est. en cela qu'il est. artiste*. Glucksmann writes in *Dostoïevski à Manhattan*: *On a dit de Dostoïevski qu'il "sent" ou "voit" les idées. C'est vrai de chaque écrivain authentique, don't la liberté de plume et d'esprit tient dans le primat de la perception sur la deduction*; English: "it has been said of Dostoevsky that he 'feels' or 'sees' ideas," (259), and he continues: "This is true of all authentic writers, whose freedom of pen and of spirit hinges on the primacy of perception over deduction" (my translation).

39. Myftiu, *Nietzsche & Dostoïevski éducateurs*, 11 (my translation): *Nietzsche et Dostoïevski. Incompatibles, peut-être, au premier abord. Semblables, au deuxième. Indépendamment du fait que l'un est considéré comme philosophe et l'autre comme écrivain, je qualifierai Nietzsche de philosophe qui écrit de la poésie et Dostoïevski de romancier qui écrit de la philosophie. Le sens contraire est également vrai. La philosophie rejoint l'art. L'art rejoint la philosophie*.

40. Nietzsche, WM [794], 523: (my translation): *Unsere Religion, Moral und Philosophie sind décadence-Formen des Menschen. Die* Gegenbewegung: *die Kunst*.

41. Nietzsche, WLN, 11[99] 216f.; "Kritik des Nihilism," KSA 13, 11[99](351) 46–9.

42. Courtine, entry "Res," 894; *Vocabulaire européen des philosophies: dictionaire des intraduisibles*.

43. Clemens and Chris Feik emphasize the role of Nechaev as a both historical and "conceptual figure" (Deleuze and Guattari, *What Is Philosophy?* 61ff.) for nihilism (together with "Nietzsche") in "Nihilism, Tonight…" in *Nihilism Now*, 32.

44. Coetzee, *The Master of Petersburg*; cf. Adelman, *Retelling Dostoevsky*, 143–50.

45. Nechaev, *Catechism of a Revolutionist*, www.uoregon.edu/~kimball/Nqv.catechism.

46. Goodwin, *Confronting Dostoevsky's Demons*, 18; See also Saraskina, *Бесы: Роман предупреждение*, 325–39.

47. See for example, Mochulsky, *Dostoevsky, His Life and Work*, 254: "The underground man's confession is the philosophical preface to the cycle of the great novels"; *Достоевский, жизнь и творчество*, 210; cf. Jackson, *The Art of Dostoevsky*, 11.

48. Shestov, *Dostoevsky and Nietzsche* (my translation); *La philosophie de la tragédie*, 72; *Достоевский и Ницше*, 36.

49. Shestov, *Dostoevsky and Nietzsche* (my translation); *La philosophie de la tragédie*, 72; *Достоевский и Ницше*, 36: *нет иного пути к истине, как через каторгу, подземелье, подполье...*

50. Dostoevsky, NU, 33. ЗП, vol. 2, 632: *ведь дважды два четыре есть уже не жизнь … а начало смерти.*

51. Dostoevsky, NU, 31; ЗП, vol. 2, 631.

52. Dostoevsky, NU, 28; ЗП, vol. 2, 628.

53. Dostoevsky, NU, 129–30; ЗП, vol. 2, 698–9.

54. Ibid. For an excellent intellectual-historical analysis of the humiliation of the "naïve optimism about the power of reason," in the *Notes from Underground*, see Nemcová Banerjee, *Dostoevsky: The Scandal of Reason*, 31–78.

55. Dostoyevsky, ЗМД, 254; HD (2015) 252; HD (2004) 209.

56. Dostoevsky, ЗМД, 27; HD (2015), 9; HD (2004) 5.

57. (My translation) 259: *On a dit de Dostoïevski qu'il "sent" ou "voit" les idées.*

58. Dostoevsky, D, 236; Б, 205.

59. Dostoevsky, D, 95; Б, 93.

60. See Adelman's analysis of Kirillov's character in terms of Nietzsche's metamorphosis of the spirit in his *Retelling Dostoevsky*, 57.

61. Dostoevsky, D, 402; Б, 334.

62. See Cox, "Kirillov, Stavrogin, and Suicide," 80.

63. Dostoevsky, D, 239; Б, 207.

64. Dostoevsky, D, 621; Б, 505; it is perhaps a mockery of Herzen, see his *Дневник писателя*, 83–4.

65. See Camus, *Myth of Sisyphus*, 108; *Le myth de Sisyphe*, 145.

66. Dostoevsky, D, 238; Б, 206. Cf. Hingley, *The Undiscovered Dostoevsky*, 160–1.

67. Dostoevsky, D, 619; Б, 503; see Paperno, *Suicide as a Cultural Institution in Dostoevsky's Russia*, 146.

68. (my translation); Б, 500: *Я всю жизнь не хотел, чтоб это только слова.*

69. Camus, *Myth of Sisyphus* 109, 111; *Le myth de Sisyphe* 145.
70. Camus, *Le myth de Sisyphe*, 145. *Myth of Sisyphus* 109: "an indescribable spiritual adventure."
71. Dostoevsky, D, 237; Б, 206; Camus, *Myth of Sisyphus*, 109: "all is well"; *Le myth de Sisyphe*, 145: *tout est bien*; in an interview, Camus said that *Biesy*, and thus his own faithful adaptation of it, "begins as a comedy, continues in a dramatic atmosphere, and ends in an atmosphere of tragedy"—Camus, "Les Possédés et le nihilisme," the interview from 01.23.1959, http://www.ina.fr/video/100016140.
72. Davison, *Camus: The Challenge of Dostoevsky*, 66.
73. Dostoevsky, D, 616; Б, 501.
74. Cicovacki, *Dostoevsky and the Affirmation of Life*, 136.
75. Real (*действительный*) exists "in fact, in praxis" (*на деле*) as opposed to existing "only in words" (*только на словах*)—see В. В. Виноградов, История слов, http://wordhist.narod.ru/, статья "*действительность, действительный*."
76. Dostoevsky, D, 615; Б, 500.
77. Cicovacki, *Dostoevsky*, 136.
78. Bulgakov, "Русская Трагедиа" 503: *Верховенский остается совершенно последователен и искренен и в своей лживости, и в своем авантюризме, и в своей отваге, которой нельзя же отрицать,—он служит своей идее. И если он ужасен и даже омерзителен, то потому, что ужасна его идея* (my translation).
79. Dostoevsky, D, 604, 606; Б, 492, 493.
80. Dostoevsky, D, 418; Б, 346; one might think of Nietzsche's notion of "Platonism for the people."
81. Dostoevsky, D, 614; Б, 500.
82. Dostoevsky, D, 421; Б, 348.
83. Dostoevsky, D, 420; Б, 348; later, Kirillov will call him a "political crook and intriguer" (*политический обманщик и интриган*)—Б, 500; D, 615.
84. Dostoevsky, D, 419; Б, 347.
85. Dostoevsky, D, 423; Б, 350.
86. Knapp, *The Annihilation of Inertia*, 110; see Dostoevsky, D, 563; Б, 460; see also NU, 18: "The result: a soap bubble, and inertia"; ЗП, 621: *В результате: мыльный пузырь и инерция*.
87. Shestov, *Speculation and Revelation*, 160; *Умозрение и откровение*, 186–7.
88. Knapp, *The Annihilation of Inertia*, 102–30.
89. Ibid., 129–30.
90. Seneca, *Eistulae Morales*. Vol. II, 71: *honestius mori discumt homines quam occidere*, 70.
91. Dostoevsky, Б, 214; D, 247.
92. Dostoevsky, D, 253; Б, 219.
93. This was at least the opinion of both Nietzsche and Camus.
94. Dostoevsky, Б, 501; D, 616.
95. The Russian says: "*Ставрогин если верует, то не верует, что он верует. Если же не верует, то не верует, что он не верует.*"
96. Nietzsche, "Nachlaß 1887–1889," in KSA 13, 144.
97. Camus, *Le myth de Sisyphe*, 91.

98. Camus, *The Myth of Sisyphus*, 66.
99. Dostoevsky, D, 676; Б, 548 (translation modified). On the lack of believe of Stavrogin as the lack of love see S.I. Gessen, *Трагедия зла*, 668–82.
100. Dostoevsky, D, 673; Б, 546.
101. Dostoevsky, D, 235 f.; Б, 204.
102. Dostoevsky, NU, 126–7. ЗП, 696: *я цделал эты жестокость, хоть нарочно, но не от сердца, а от дурной моией головы......Эта жестокость была до того напускная, до того головная, нарочно подсочиненная, книжная, что я сам не выдержал даже минуты.*
103. Ibid. 124/695: *но ведь рассуждениями ничего не объяснишь, а следствен но, и рассуждать нечего.*
104. Nietzsche, GM (1989) III [1], 97 and [28], 163; *Zur Genealogie der Moral*, in *KSA* 5, III [1], 339 and [28], 412: "*lieber will noch der Mensch* das Nichts *wollen, als* nicht *wollen...*"; cf. III [14] 122; *KSA* 5, III [14] 368, and Owen and Aaron Ridley interpretation in their "Dramatis Personae," 149.
105. Knapp, *The Annihilation of the Inertia*, 116–17.
106. Life means here "the will to will" (*Wille zum Willen*), writes Heidegger, interpreting Nietzsche, in *Off the Beaten Track*, 176; *Holzwege*, 235; cf. Nietzsche, WP, 1017; KSA 12 10[5](140) 456–7.
107. Ivanov (Вячеслав Иванов), "Достоевский и роман-трагедия," Кн. 5, 46–61, 165: *вера и неверие не два различных объяснения мира или два различных руководительства в жизни, но два разноприродных бытия* (my translation).
108. Nietzsche analyses this conversation between Kirillov and Vierchovensky, with other references to Stavrogin, in his *Nachlaß 1887–1889*, KSA 13, 11[331]-[351], 141–53.
109. Dostoevsky, D, 688; Б, 557.
110. Dostoevsky, DW, vol. I, 539 (my emphasis); ДП, 360; almost one century later, Camus defined nihilism as "the emptiness of heart, the impossibility of arriving at any faith or belief"—Camus "*The Possessed* and the nihilism." *Le vide du cœur, l'impossibilitée d'adhérer à une foi ou une croyance quelconque*—"*Les Possédés* et le nihilisme" the interview from 01.28.1959, http://www.ina.fr/video/100016140.
111. Dostoevsky, D, 619; Б, 503: *uverovat', chto ne veriu*; Kirillov's admiration for Christ is based on this same affirmation of the "divine humanity" of faith. It is presented as a "big idea" (*большая идея*), an exact opposition to Verhovensky's "little idea" (*идейка*)—Dostoevsky, D, 618; Б, 502; cf. Heidegger's interpretation of Nietzsche's affirmation of the will to will, in *Nietzsche* IV [Eng.] 31; *Nietzsche* II [Ger.] 54.
112. Brzoza radically opposes the two suicides to each other: the "energetic" (*energiczny*) gesture of shooting, and the "passive" (*bierne*) hanging on the rope, according to the law of inertia (*prawo inercji*)—Halina Brzoza, *Dostojewski między mitem, tragedia i apokalipsą*, 173.
113. Nietzsche, WP [435], 239; KSA 13, 14[94], 272; cf. KSA 5, I [12] 278; GM, I (1989) [12] 44.

Chapter 3

Purification of Cruelty in Antonin Artaud

"Artaud kept himself as close as possible to the limit: the possibility and impossibility of pure theater."[1] Jacques Derrida celebrated thus the work of Antonin Artaud. Artaud was also the one who actually opposed culture, or civilization, to cruelty. The former, currently in crisis, needs the latter in order to not only maintain itself, but to progress and blossom, to draw from it the force of life: "What is most important, it seems to me is not so much to defend a culture whose existence has never kept a man from going hungry, as to extract, from what is called culture, ideas whose compelling force is identical with that of hunger."[2] Hunger, desire, or cruelty, the primal forces of life (*cruor*—blood) should play a crucial role in the f/act of culture. As Derrida writes, quoting Artaud: "*Le théâtre de la cruauté n'est pas une représentation. C'est la vie elle-même en ce qu'elle a d'irreprésentable. La vie est l'origine non représentable de la représentation. "J'ai donc dit 'cruauté' comme j'aurais dit 'vie'.*"[3] Hunger and cruelty should unite what was artificially disjoint. Artaud's critique of modern Western culture is as harsh as that of Nietzsche's. In most general terms, it is characterized by "a rupture between things and words, between things and the ideas and signs that are their representation."[4] This culture is that of indifferent spectatorship (Aristotle's *theatēs*—spectator, quintessence of the theoretical man, Artaud's "pipping Tom"—*voyeur*). Words acquired a separate status, an ideological, rhetorical force, independent of their magical involvement with things. Artaud has a primary physical abhorrence of Western culture, which he associates with the white color of the skin: "we (Europeans) give off an odor as white as gathering of pus in an infected wound. As iron can be heated until it turns white, so it can be said that everything excessive is white; for Asians white has become the mark of extreme decomposition."[5] White is also the color of indifference, of white-washing the colors of life. The characterization of our culture is that of indifference. "To our disinterested and inert idea of art an authentic culture opposes a violently egoistic and magical, i.e., *interested* idea."[6] Authentic culture, that is, "culture-in-action" rejects indifference, and on the contrary, promotes difference: "This difference or determination as such is also cruelty."[7] "Cruelty is nothing but determination *as such*, that precise point at which the determined maintains its essential relation with the undetermined, that rigorous abstract line fed by *chiaroscuro*."[8] Difference determines the singularity of being, its uniqueness in respect to other beings. It does not consider difference from the outside, as it were, formally, transcendentally, at a certain distance. It is this comfortable distance from reality that Artaud suspects of destroying our culture. As Nietzsche, Artaud rejects the "systematic" culture, the "systems of thought," "their number and contradictions characterize our old French and European culture: but where can it be shown that life, our life, has ever been affected by these systems?"[9] The answer to this rhetorical question is, of course, "nowhere," and the response to the conundrum lies in the so-called "culture-in-action," that Artaud promotes, or the "uncanny spectacle."

What was seductive in the Sirens' song? According to Maurice Blanchot, the strangeness of their voice, properly inhuman, or rather, the familiarity of their singing, usual singing of human beings, that Sirens imitated perfectly and which combined with their bestial nature, rendered the concert so uncanny, that suspicions arose among the listeners of "the inhumanity of all human song."[10] From those two points of view on the nature of enchantment, it is not the first which renders this phenomenon disturbing: the danger could be determined, and fought off effectively, as in the case of Ulysses,[11] by wisdom, by craftiness, by persuasion, and the communal discipline. But if it is the other cause of the effect of Sirens' song which were true? How to protect the human in the case of the absence of clearly delimited territory.

ARISTOTELIAN AND ARTAUDIAN CATHARSIS

The cruelty is generally defined as the lack of the human sentiment, the lack of what Aristotle called *philanthropon*—the sentiment of kindness for those who are not equal to us. Cruel act is the act of cowardice practiced toward the weak. One thinks about torture, about mindless slaughter, about gratuitous infliction of suffering. One thinks, with etymology of shed blood (*cruor*), of bloody flesh (*kreas*). Cruelty is a negation of human and of rational. For someone who believes in the supreme value of the human—a humanist—the cruelty should be contained: condemned as criminal or diagnosed as a psychic deviation, a sickness—the sadism—and edged out. Like Ulysses who was listening to the Sirens' song without danger, being firmly attached by his companions to the mast of the ship, the humanist could contemplate the disturbing spectacle only if his poetic base were solid, if he disposed of the mechanisms of purification or of expulsion of the phenomenon of cruelty, in other words, if he disposed of the framing doctrine, establishing the borders and their guard. The word which traditionally designated such a mechanism of containment was called *catharsis*. It is much older than Aristotle's *Poetics*, but it was his catharsis that influenced occidental humanism, well beyond the literature or the theater and well beyond the classical age *sensu stricto*.

The "end" (*telos*) of the tragedy is "through pity and fear accomplishing the catharsis of such emotions."[12] Probably it does not exist in occidental literature another phrase which could compete with this as to the multitude and variety of its interpretations. There is, however, a kernel which could be hardly disputed, the de*limitation* of cases deserving of pity and of fear (*eleeina kai phobera*), that is to say the elimination of the inhuman from the world of tragedy. The spectacle of brutality, of the suffering of innocents, of crime, especially the successful crime, do not incite at all the fear and pity—the sentiments of solidarity—but incite, on the contrary, the disgust (*miaron*)—the sentiment of rejection.[13] Also the free spectacle of horror, the spectacle which is not justified by plot (*muthos*) is to be eliminated from tragic art as monstrosity (*teratôdes*).[14] At least, this is the interpretation of Lessing in his *Hamburgische Dramaturgie*. He even adduces the example of such disgusting action in Christian Felix Weisse's *Richard the Third*, which is opposed to Shakespeare's play of the same title, as the one exceeding in terms of cruelty the possibilities of catharsis. Lessing's text had an immense influence on modern, neo-classical theater, and it is this theater that Brecht opposed when he called his theater "non-cathartic theater" or "non-Aristotelian theater." Artaud's theater does not follow the pattern of brecht. On the contrary, he reacts specially against the "Enlightenment side of Brecht" (Althusser),[15] against estranging distance of the spectators toward the spectacle. Even though Brecht characterizes his theater as "praxis in the theater" there is a theorist's, spectator's attitude in it; we should learn from the characters' actions, and not identify with them.

Thus, for Aristotle, theater essentially plays a conservative role in the education ordained by the State, one from which an unlimited range of social metamorphoses should be excluded.[16] The ghost of the dangerous theater that Plato feared has been exorcised, or rather purified in the figure of *pharmakos*, hero, criminal, and victim at the same time.[17] It is, indeed, the institution of catharsis that plays the crucial part in the submission of theater to the philosophical rule.[18] Aristotle's "purified" theater becomes the instrument of choice in the educative/ideological task of consecrating the ideal social types. The respect for the separation between world and theater and between stage and auditorium constitutes the beginning and principle *(arkhê)* of the order of catharsis.

This form of philosophical theater unfolded during the neoclassical period. The "Cartesian" and "Academic" spirit of the seventeenth century eventually spelled out the rapprochement of philosophy and theater in the wake of Aristotle's *Poetics*. It produced the world of order and became even more philosophical than Aristotle, the Philosopher, wanted it to be. The rules of "the three unities," of verisimilitude, decorum, separation of genres, poetic justice, and catharsis, have made the neoclassical theater the model of an ordered universe.

Ulysses' wax and ropes would not be effective against Sirens' song, if we interpreted it as the inhuman within the human. The mechanism of the catharsis and the limitations of fear and pity could not separate "absolute danger" from the cruelty which is in the heart of the real, according to Antonin Artaud and in the heart of his poetics. The cruelty of which Artaud talks is not "vulgar, vicious cruelty." If this is not absent from the spectacle of cruelty, it is because it revels the fragility of all forms of limitations. It is, by the way, only "a very minor aspect of the question."[19] The "true" cruelty is, according to Artaud, a cosmic force, a necessary principle of life and creation, an energy of which theatrical act will be the revelation: "It is not a question of always brandishing a butcher's knife on the stage, but of reintroducing in every theatrical gesture the notion of a kind of cosmic cruelty without which there would be neither life nor reality."[20] The cruelty is not an element unknown to being, it is in the root (source) of life and the theater.

Artaud's "terror and cruelty" appears to make allusion to Aristotle's "terror (the frequent translation of *phobos*) and pity (*eleos*)." It is striking, that Artaud as well as Aristotle, links both terms with the notion of purification. Would it be justified to talk, with Franco Tonelli[21] about "Artaudian catharsis"? Can we employ the same term for designating the conceptions so different without risking their confusion? Artaud talks about "extreme purification." We should understand this word not only in opposition with *mêden agan* ("nothing too much") of classic humanism, but also, and especially, as referring to "borders," to "limits," to "the strange" and to "the stranger," to "the external," as suggests etymology of "extreme": *in extremis, out of limits*. The superlative *extreme* often used by Artaud regarding cruel action involves also the dynamic idea of tension toward the exterior, the idea of excess, of transcendence. Its poetics is an aesthetic thematization of the concept of *limits* in general, which is also a questioning of *the limits of the human, cruel*. The "unusual ideas" to which the Theater of Cruelty has to appeal to merit its name, have a particularity that they "cannot be limited or even formally depicted."[22] "Everything that acts is a cruelty" he writes "it is upon this idea of extreme action, pushed beyond all limits, that theater must be rebuilt."[23]

The cruel song will be fascinating because it will lead till beyond the borders of the human, but will not have anything exotic, because it is in man himself that it will find them. The preface to *The Theater and Its Double* explicitly names the borders to *de-fine* (in the sense of *un-limit*): the Theater of Cruelty has to aim at "the rejection of the usual limitations of man and man's powers, and infinitely extends the frontiers of what is called reality."[24] From the practical side it means the rejection of psychological analyses of moralistic typology of the theater of characters, for the sake of spectacle of musical vibrations, of light, of dance, or the poetry of free gesture of forces which "sweeps away human individuality."[25]

The analogy with plague is certainly the most striking illustration of crossing all the limits, a rupture of all human bonds. The experience of epidemic is instructive as the extreme case where precisely the idea of human solidarity should be confirmed, as it happens in Albert Camus' *The Plague*. According to Artaud often it is the opposite that happens: in such circumstances, the community of *philanthropia* turns out to be an illusion, the city and family collapses, the cruelty appears. In "The Theater and the Plague" Artaud cites the cases which show the social disintegration during the epidemic, disintegration equal to the plague-stricken body: the disorder becomes established. The gratuitous acts, the crimes, the excesses are committed, even in the interior of families: "the obedient and virtuous son kills his father; the chaste man performs sodomy upon his kin . . . the warrior hero sets fire to the city he once risked his life to save."[26] On the other hand, the people become virtuous: "the lecher becomes pure. The miser throws his gold in handfuls out the window."[27] "Criminals," "virtuous"? The plague shows the fragility of these *determinations* of the *ethno-centric* anthropology in case of crisis. The function of the theater will be to remake this demystifying experience to put us on guard against instability of the borders of the human, to show that "the sky can still fall on our heads."[28] The process of this rise of awareness will be the Artaudien "purification."

The "extreme purification" is considered by Artaud as the only alternative to death, as well in total crises of plague as of the theater of cruelty. Salutary effect of the two experiences is a spiritual recognition. But it is neither the Aristotelian *anagnôrisis*, nor Brechtian recognition of the social conditions of life, both, at the end reassuring their cosmo- and anthropo-logic vision. It is rather the individual and collective taking awareness of the condition of universal cruelty, of "suffocating inertia of the matter," of irremediable chaos, of the impulses and of the passions on the one hand, and also of this exciting "dark power," of "hidden force" on the other hand. They invite they who "experience" the plague and the theater "to take, in the face of destiny, a superior and heroic attitude they would never have assumed without it."[29] In fact, the result of the plague (and analogically of the "cruel" theater) is not only negative—the diagnostic of fragility of human's authority—but also positive—the discovery of otherwise unsuspected forces:

> A social disaster so far-reaching, an organic disorder so mysterious—this overflow of vices, this total exorcism which presses and impels the soul to its utmost—all indicate the presence of a state which is nevertheless characterized by extreme strength and in which all the powers of nature are freshly discovered at the moment when something essential is going to be accomplished.[30]

One has to note in this text, apart from the expressions already considered of luminary experience, the word *exorcism*, which conjugate this experience (*herkos*—barrier, closure) with that of spiritual liberation.

However the result of this "passing by crises" is not here, like in case of Aristotelian catharsis, the quiet return to the interior of limits reassuring the human world, but on the contrary, crossing of borders toward dangerous world of cruel forces: the "essential theater," like the plague, is "the revelation, the bringing forth, the exteriorization of the depth of latent cruelty."[31] This depth of latent cruelty nourishes, according to Artaud, as well the world of inert matter, as that of living bodies and the passions individual and collective. The world—cosmos—is cruel "from the point of view of our existence," that is to say, it is perceived as an obstacle to the realization of our will. The cruelty is the "cosmic rigor," the "necessity" when it is seen as the "implacable intention and decision, irreversible and absolute determination."[32] Thus, in the strict sense, the word "cruelty" designates in Artaud a state of real lucidity and of submission to the necessity which characterizes the tragic hero. "There is no cruelty without consciousness and without the application of consciousness."[33] "Applied," that is to say, bringing to action. The submission to the necessity does not mean passive acceptance of fate, but on the contrary, the struggle, the revolt, the transfiguration, the transcendence of limits of established order, that is to say, the creation. The theater of cruelty will be the continuous expression of this creation: "A play in which there would not be this will, this blind appetite for life capable of overriding everything, visible in each gesture and each act and in the transcendent aspect of the story, would be a useless and unfulfilled play."[34] *Annabella*[35] by Ford is certainly not such a play. On the contrary, it is, for Artaud, the model of the *transcendence of action*. Incestuous love, defiance of ecclesiastic and familiar authority, of laws, the provocation of the slaughter in the last scene, when Giovanni arrives to the banquet with the extracted heart of his sister, to affronts not only his rival but the human order in its foundation, is the image of supreme cruelty as the "absolute of revolt." Artaud describes the progress of action in terms belonging to the esthetic of the sublime: anarchic progress "from excess to excess" is also the *elevation*. The cruel hero stands "beyond vengeance, beyond crime, by still another crime, one that is indescribably passionate; beyond threats, beyond horror by an ever greater horror."[36] The apogee of cruelty is here the expression of the sublime, superhuman love.

The terror follows necessarily this exaltation of anarchic freedom, which is also the vertigo of abyss—abyss of the inhuman. It is hero's terror, like Beatrice from Artaud's play *The Cenci*, who dies with anguish of contagion of cruelty.

> Oh, my eyes, what a dreadful vision you will see as you die. How can I be sure that, down there, I shall not be confronted by my father? The very notion makes my death more bitter. For I fear that my death may teach me that I have ended by resembling him.[37]

It is also the terror of spectator, which precisely ceases to be the spectator; it is the terror of participation in the cruel spectacle. The difference with the Aristotelian *phobos* is a difference of modes of discourse: "this could have happened to us" would say the spectators of classic theater: "this is happening to us" would say (if they have the leisure) the "participants" of the theater of cruelty. The sentiment of absolute danger, of "terror" is a direct consequence of cruel reality of the scenic events. The theater of Artaud is not a *mimesis*, in the sense of the representation, of the copy of some events which happened elsewhere—*alibi*. The limits of humanity, in which we believe to be secure, are traversed in our presence. In fact it is we who are crossing them: "after an instant the magic identification is made: WE KNOW IT IS WE WHO WERE SPEAKING."[38] This 'we" does not send back to the community of compassion, of fear and of *philanthropon*, but on the contrary, and paradoxically, to the immediate experience of anguish of abyss of all these who recognize their voices in the Sirens' song. Artaud calls this immersion in the abyss of cruelty in the case of Heliogabalus "crowned anarchy."

CRUELTY AND ANARCHY

It is Matthew Arnold who famously opposed culture and anarchy. He described the actuality of culture, based on a rational belief in its steady progress. For Artaud, contrary to Arnold, anarchy has a positive value, especially in its relation to culture. Yet, he combines the sense of cultural unity with anarchy. Heliogabalus, his hero and alter ego, is able to respect at the same time the profound unity of things and their diversity: Heliogabalus "in so far as he was king, found himself in the best possible position to reduce human multiplicity and restore it through blood, cruelty and war to the sense of unity."[39] Monotheism, which symbolizes this sense of unity, should yield to the sense of anarchy: "it's the monotheism, the universal unity, which obstructs mere impulse and the multiplicity of things, which *I* call anarchy"[40] It is as a creator of unity that anarchy is "at the root of all poetry." It is "anarchic to the degree that it brings into play all the relationships of object to object and of form to signification. It is anarchic also to the degree that its occurrence is the consequence of a disorder that draws us closer to chaos."[41] This formula evokes the "idea of chaos." The expression "idea of chaos" seems as paradoxical, from the Platonic perspective, as the "unified order of anarchy" does. Indeed, *Ideai* are the principles of order in Plato's metaphysics, cosmology, and politics; they are paradigms of the order of representation, excluding the possibility of chaos. In Plato, poetry and theater defy order, especially the order of the city (i.e., justice), by blurring the distinction between social types (*tupoi*), which are based on Ideas. By impersonating (*mimeisthai*) a person from another type or class, for example, or by identifying with a different character on the stage, one risks really becoming (*einai*) such a person or character, at least according to Socrates in Plato's *Republic*. One risks crossing the boundary between appearance and reality, introducing confusion and undermining the basis of the political order.[42] Consequently, there is no place for theater in the ideal world of *The Republic*; the threat of confusion is to great; the tenth book of *The Republic* demands the banishment of the poet, principally the tragic poet, from the city—a gesture that has marked the whole history of both Western theater and Western philosophy of art.[43]

Although Artaud's phrase "idea of chaos" and his "idea of becoming" and of the "marvelous" which appear in one of the programmatic essays for his "theater of cruelty," probably do not refer directly to Plato's metaphysical *Ideas*, they most certainly return to his notion of a "dangerous theater."[44] After centuries dominated by the Aristotelian model of the "cathartic theater," Artaud returns to the Platonic notion of the theater as a threat to the metaphysical and political order, as a danger. At the same time, he proposes to confer on the "theater of cruelty" the task reserved for philosophy in *The Republic*, that is, of apprehending the world and of providing guidance for the action in the world. The "theater of cruelty" ought to realize a "metaphysics-in-action" *(métaphysique en activité)*,[45] which of course evokes "culture-in-action" (*culture en action*).[46]

Indeed, a stage of violence might provide, in Augusto Boal's view of the theater of action, a "rehearsal for the revolution."[47] From Aeschylus' *Prometheus Bound* and Sophocles' *Antigone* to Genet's *Balcony* and Weiss/ Brooks' *Marat/Sade*, Western theater portrays, analyzes, and perhaps "rehearses" revolutionary situations. If other literary forms and arts engage in making and unmaking worlds, they do it less "dramatically" for they are further removed from direct action in the political community. The role of theater in this respect is privileged because of its inherently social character and its paradigmatic status of *représentation* (performance/ representation).

A particular form of representation symbolizes and governs a particular political, artistic, and scientific world order.

Aristotle's intervention in the ancient quarrel between philosophy and poetry is far from beneficial for the latter. To be sure, theater is recalled from exile, but on what terms? It is now integrated into the rational system of representation with well-defined boundaries. The world is a world, and the theater is a theater; there is no danger of confusing the two. The relationship between the world of the stage and the world of the spectators is cast as resemblance *(homoiosis)*, which is distinctly separated from identity. Even the most exact imitation cannot have the same effect as the real.[48] Aristotle's mimesis is not a play *(paidia)* with the limits of reality and illusion, as in Plato; rather it is the education *(paideia)* of adults already aware of their place, their status in the social structure of the city. Theater reinforces this structure. The characters on the stage should conform to established types, differentiated according to their virtue and power.[49] The queens and kings in a tragedy are portrayed as "better than ourselves," and characters in a comedy as worse. We should not completely identify with them, but only empathize with their vulnerability to *hamartiai* or faults—mostly offenses against the political and religious laws—in order to become aware of our own vulnerability in the same respect.

Artaud's "theater of cruelty" challenges this model, which has dominated the Western stage since the seventeenth century and still dominates most of the *théâtre de boulevard* and Broadway theater. However, Artaud's challenge is not limited to the world of theater narrowly understood. It pertains to the whole Western philosophical *Weltanschauung*, to its contemplative, purely intellectual kind of philosophy. Artaud restored to the idea of world-as-theater the philosophical disquiet of certain Baroque plays. In Artaud's project, *theatrum mundi* definitively lost the security of a rhetorical figure, of a *"lieu commun de l'humanisme."* If the world is a "theater of cruelty," as Artaud suggests, it becomes an anarchic, evil, and cruel world, resistant to the philosophical "cosmodicy."

In Plato, theater is rejected as a threat to the purity of the ideal contemplation. In Aristotle, theater is rehabilitated because it is shown to be able to uphold the principle of the philosophical contemplation of the real and the boundary of the sensible and the intelligible. Theater is philosophical to the extent that it extracts the general *(ta katholou)* from the particular *(ta kath'hekaston)*. Sensuous spectacle is dispensable when the intelligible reality of *ta katholou* is presented through plot *(muthos* or *logos*—the "soul of tragedy"): "Spectacle is emotionally potent but falls outside the art and is not integral to poetry." Aristotle writes that the effect of tragedy does not depend on its performance by actors.[50]

Artaud implicitly refers to this statement and to the one concerning the full tragic effect of a simple reading (or listening to) the plot of *Oedipus the King* when he complains that for "certain theatrical amateurs . . . a play read affords just as definite and as great a satisfaction as the same play performed."[51] This "greater satisfaction" *(des joies autrement grandes)*[52] of the classical, philosophical theater results from the repression of the sensuous spectacle that might impair the contemplation of the formal purity of *logos*. The ideality of *logos* (word, plot)[53] is in need of definition, that is, of separation between the fixed master text and the "aesthetics of the stage."[54] However, such an aesthetic of the fixed text, with a "clear and distinct" meaning, leads necessarily to its own perversion, as Artaud asserts: "The obsession with the defined word which says everything ends in the withering of words *(dessèchement des mots)*."[55] The aesthetics of cruelty will try to break with the verbose theater not in order to suppress words altogether, but in order to rediscover under the dead, frozen rhetoric of the fixed meaning the vital motion of words and gestures "humming with significations *(bourdonnantes de signification)*."[56] In order to convey his idea of language in the theater, Artaud resorts to the Platonic and Baroque rapprochement between theater and dream: "It is not a question of suppression of the articulated word, but of giving to words approximately the importance they have in dreams."[57]

The movements of words should not appear as isolated units of meaning. As in the Oriental, Balinese theater admired by Artaud, they are to expand beyond themselves in the space, transpose words into cries, groans, incantations so as to perform a "vibratory action upon the sensibility," so as to "exalt, to benumb, to charm, to arrest."[58] These movements are accompanied by all other motions of the stage: actors' gestures, dance, plastic images, music, light, all merging into a total spectacle. "Exorcism" is the word Artaud uses in order to characterize the effect of such a theater; and what is eventually exorcised here is the "intellectual subjugation of the language." Both the means and the effect of the language—the site of *logos* and of *idea* in the classical theater—are to be marked in Artaud's theater by the "aesthetic" world of sensibility.

The abolition of "the barrier of speech," that is, the barrier protecting the ideality of the pure *logos* from contamination by the physical expression, brings with it the elimination of all other protective barriers *(les gardes-fous)* of the ideology of the classical stage.[59] The stage itself, as a space separated from the auditorium, loses its *raison d'être*. If the spectator is placed in the center of the spectacle ("in the 'theater of cruelty' the spectator is in the center and the spectacle surrounds him"),[60] it is not in order to control the world of the spectacle but, on the contrary, in order to be sensuously overcome by it:

> It is in order to attack the spectator's sensibility on all sides that we advocate a revolving spectacle which, instead of making the stage and auditorium two closed worlds *(deux mondes clos)*, without possible communication, spreads its visual and sonorous outbursts over the entire mass of the spectators.[61]

Such an intense, direct stimulation of all the senses of the body resembles Dionysian experiences of trances that forestall in their participants all distancing gestures and force upon them a total identification with the synaesthetic spectacle, produced by gesture, word, sound, music, and combinations of these.[62] The "cruel" spectacle liberates the "life which sweeps away human individuality and in which man is only a reflection."[63] The limits of the auditorium where the spectators of the classical theater felt secure are crossed; in fact, the spectators of the "theater of cruelty" recognize themselves: *"Nous savons que c'est nous qui parlions"* (we know it is we who were speaking).[64]

Artaud's aesthetics, concerned as it is with the effect of *synaesthesia*—a "collusion of objects, silences, shouts, and rhythms"[65]—may be more properly called *"synaesthetics."* However, the *synaesthesia* of the theater of cruelty is not an exclusively sensuous phenomenon. For Artaud, the essential boundary between the intelligible and the sensible is no longer binding. This interplay of different aesthetic, sensuous, and spiritual images overwhelms the spectators and produces in them a total identification with actors and characters, thus realizing a magic transformation comparable to the one the actor Genest of Rotrou's play accomplished on a personal level.[66] This is a religious idea of theater, a dangerous idea too, as the court of the emperor Diocletian correctly perceived. The order of the (political and aesthetic) world can no longer be guaranteed when the boundaries between illusion and reality, between acting and action, that is, between theater and life, are crossed. The danger is, of course, multiplied when the characters are "crowned anarchists." The "identification" in the "theater of cruelty" differs from Aristotle's notion of *eleos* and Lessing's notion of *Mitleid* (both usually translated as "pity" or "empathy"), in which the spectators adhere to the order represented by the heroes (the one they break while still accepting it and rejecting the chaos of the monsters). Both acceptance and rejection confirm the moral order shared by the characters and the audience. In the theater of cruelty, on the other hand, even when particular characters are maintained, the order is threatened. Indeed, the identification with Cenci, a Giovanni, a Heliogabalus, produces a disarray rather than a comfortable sense of order.[67] They are all "crowned anarchists," although only the latter is called thus explicitly. And Heliogabalus is not even a consistent anarchist, like Aristotle's "consistently inconsistent" (*homalos anomalon*) character.[68]

FIERY PURIFICATION

A strange rhythm intervenes in Heliogabalus' cruelty; this initiate does everything with art and everything in double. I mean everything on two planes. Each of his gestures is double-edged.

Order, Disorder,
Unity, Anarchy,
Poetry, Dissonance,
Rhythm, Discordance,
Grandeur, Puerility,
Generosity, Cruelty.[69]

Far from producing an effect of harmony, as did the Pythagorean binary oppositions cited by Aristotle, the doubles of the typical Artaudian hero lead to the questioning of any order and to the collapse of meaning. Artaud himself recognizes the risk of an audience's total identification with the anarchic characters. He anticipates some of the criticism directed against the theater of cruelty: "It will be claimed," he writes in the essay "No More Masterpieces," "that example breeds example, that if the attitude of cure induces cure, the attitude of murder will induce murder." The language of Artaud's answer to this criticism might provoke some misunderstandings if not referred to his clearer statements in other texts. Artaud's view should be understood neither in the sense of aestheticism, which he often repudiates elsewhere,[70] nor in the sense of the classical Aristotelian catharsis.[71] Whereas for Aristotle "[t]he world of tragic events must . . . be rational," and "the world *[tout court]* remains a rational, meaningful place,"[72] for Artaud, as for Plato, the two worlds are in danger of confusion with one another.

Yet, for Artaud, this "idea of chaos"—intoxicating and dangerous—gives the theater a certain epistemological, in the sense of "apocalyptic," quality. The task of the "theater of cruelty" is to impart to the audience a sense of anarchy, both liberating and perilous. At the same time, it produces enough energy for challenging the established order of the world and a revelation *(apokalupsis)* of the truth of the human condition, namely, that *"nous ne sommes pas libres. Et le ciel peut encore nous tomber sur la tête"* ("we are not free. And the sky can still fall on our heads").[73] The "truth," the idea of chaos, cannot be conveyed in a rational way because it consists precisely in the collapse of rationality. Only in a sensuous, aesthetic manner is it possible to experience the total loss of boundaries. Artaud's identification of cruelty with life—"I have . . . said 'cruelty' as I might have said 'life'"[74]—should be viewed in this apocalyptic context. The principle that allows for the highest achievements of the human spirit reveals itself in the utter dissolution of "all bounds":

> Life cannot help exercising some blind rigor that carries with it all its conditions, otherwise it would not be life; but this rigor, this life that exceeds all bounds and is exercised in the torture and trampling down of everything, this pure implacable feeling is what cruelty is.[75]

Artaud is confident that such an experience of theatrical cruelty will produce a magic transfiguration in the audience that will eventually lead to the restoration of the sense of order and to the idea of a "cosmic rigor."[76] Artaud's *"sublimation"* designates such a transformation of the spectator in the sense of an absolute generosity toward the world and toward its fragility. This generosity suggests less a Kantian passive contemplation with no interest in the existence of its object than a mimetic identification in the sense of acting-play-action, which is also a form of (aesthetic) knowing/sensing oneself in the world. Such experience profoundly marks the audience. Artaud explicitly "defies" the spectator of the theater of cruelty who has witnessed the violent spectacle "to give himself up, once *outside* theater, to ideas of war, riot, and blatant murder."[77] Thus, Artaud sees the effect of his theater in cathartic terms after all—in the modern sense of catharsis associated with sublimation: the violence of blood is eventually transformed into the "violence of thought" *(violence de la pensée)*. And the violence of thought is, as we already said, the difference as a reaction to the bourgeois nihilism of indifference. Difference in itself determines the singularity of being. It is precisely not the difference (Aristotelian *differentia specifica*), which classifies the world, bringing order, but anarchic difference, not dependent on the "tyranny of genres."

The idea of purity is a metaphysical, cosmological, political, and religious idea—an idea directed against the danger of chaos and indetermination. Any kind of pollution "offends against order."[78] The purpose of the process of purification is to establish a manageable structure, a system of distinctions, of "degrees" (in Shakespeare's Ulysses' words),[79] that would prevent a struggle of all against all. A difference of status that leads to limited tension, far from destroying the whole, the "empire," contributes to its preservation: *diuide et impera*, the Romans used to say. Various cosmological, political, and religious systems of values unite their forces in order to maintain the cosmos of differences and hierarchies. They all perform their function of connecting and cementing *(re-ligare)* the world through the rites of separation between the high and the low, the governing and the governed, the pure and the impure. Western philosophy and art, as a part of the cultural process of cathartic differentiation, has been involved in the creation of cosmic and political order. The notion of catharsis epitomizes—from Plato and Aristotle to Freud and Breuer—this involvement in the creation of order in the West.

ALCHEMICAL PURIFICATION

But there are also in the Western tradition traces of another notion of purification, a notion related to alchemical and poetic metamorphosis. This form of purification, an important idea of ancient and medieval, but also modern and modernist poetics, violates the order of strict separation of realms and thus can hardly find a place among the dominant metaphysical and aesthetic ideas. The notion of "metamorphosis" that grounds alchemical and poetic purification should not be understood as a rational concept, as another binary opposition to catharsis, but rather as a challenge to the order of binary oppositions in general—a challenge to the order of the "proper order."[80]

Plato is often considered responsible for introducing the systematic thought of purification *(katharsis)* into Western philosophical terminology. In the dialogue *Phaedo*, it is philosophy itself that Socrates considers a kind of purification *(katharôs ti eisesthai, katharôs gnônai)*,[81] a purification of the soul from sensuous experiences, and eventually the extreme purification: death. The "practice of death" *(melete thanatou)* becomes the definition of philosophy,[82] the radical de-limitation of the intelligible and the sensuous realms, the latter being rejected as the source of distraction and confusion. In another of Plato's dialogues, *The Republic*, Socrates characterizes the education of the "guardians" as "purification" *(diakathairontes, kathairômen)*.[83] What is purified in that process is again the sensuous mystification or mimesis, incarnated in art, literature, and in particular theater. A mimetic performance of actors literally introduces confusion into the system of established (social) roles or types *(tupoi):* a male enacting a female; a simple man playing a ruler, a king.[84] Consequently, art, and especially theater, are to be excluded from the Platonic well-governed state. Only the simple stories that would confirm the social division will be allowed. Socrates gives an example of such purified "anthropogony": the myth of metals. In this story humans are said to be modeled subterraneously from gold, silver, bronze, and iron.[85] Their nature and its stability is thus fixed and guaranteed by the immutability of metals. They are the closest approximation to Ideas in the sensuous realm.

Excluded not only from the ideal city by Plato but also from the Christian city by St. Augustine,[86] Western art and the theater, in apparent need of purification, find it in the notion of catharsis that became the principle of the so-called neoclassical or Aristotelian theory of theater. Indeed, Aristotle's *Poetics* has been interpreted in modern times as a response to Socrates' charge of promoting anarchy, directed toward art and the theater in *The Republic*.[87] According to this interpretation Aristotle produced in the *Poetics* a demonstration of the philosophical nature of poetry and art, and of the need for them. Like philosophy, poetry would be able to achieve its goal without engaging the senses of the body. Like philosophy, it would direct the interest of the soul toward the intelligible realm, toward the realm of *logos*. Like philosophy, it would preserve the hierarchy of social types: a man, a woman, a slave, a prince, a weaver, etc., and guard against sedition in the city.[88] Aristotle's mimesis is no longer the histrionic mystification presented in the third book of Plato's *Republic,* but rather a faithful, "probable" *(eikos, vraisemblable)* representation of the dominant political opinion *(doxa),* and of nature.[89]

Modern, avowedly "anti-Aristotelian," philosophy of the seventeenth century, far from questioning the classical model, strongly confirms it through its methodological requirement of *"notions claires et distinctes"* (clear and distinct concepts) and through radical separation ("purification") of the sensible from the intelligible realms. Descartes' distinction between *res cogitans* and *res extensa* founds anew the Platonic dualism of body and soul. It provides a modern epistemological basis for the old *sôma/sêma* (body/tomb) identification, as adopted by Plato. Again the notion of purification proves a perfect metaphor for the "thinking thing's" activity of distancing itself from the "sensory, extensive thing." Language becomes a privileged field of this philosophical activity and brings it close to the object of neoclassical art. All their differences notwithstanding, modern philosophies of language from Descartes to Wittgenstein (of the *Tractatus*) remained attached to the ideal of purity and clarity of language and thought. As far as the language of art is concerned, this ideal transcends neoclassical aesthetics. Modernist poetics and poetry—of Baudelaire, Mallarmé, Valéry, Yeats, and Eliot, and of their neo-symbolist heirs—is often preoccupied with the purification and clarification of language.[90]

Does the "Artaudian purification" have anything to do with this tradition of philosophical catharsis in the classical and modern (theory of) art and the theater?[91] One might doubt it, considering Artaud's hostility toward the "theater of masterpieces." And yet it is precisely in his programmatic essay "No More Masterpieces" that the word "purification" appears: "The theater teaches," says Artaud, "the uselessness of the action which, once done, is not to be [re]done, and the superior use of the state unused by the action and which, *restored,* produces a purification."[92] To be sure, the word "purification" can be read only in the English version of the essay; the French text has *"sublimation."*[93] But Mary Caroline Richards' free translation is perhaps not illegitimate. After all, Artaud does use the word purity in the preceding sentence. "Everything depends," he says, "upon the manner and the purity with which the thing is done."[94] The "thing" *(la chose)* refers here to the "cruel" spectacle that Artaud defends against the accusation (an accusation anticipated by Artaud and in fact raised many times since) of inducing crime through an example of a criminal attitude, that is, by provoking a mimesis or imitation of an action performed on the stage and considered to be a representation of everyday reality. The aesthetic purity postulated by Artaud is to be understood in contradistinction to this classical notion of representation of the real. The process of purification in the theater of cruelty is related neither to the Aristotelian and neoclassical notion of catharsis and mimesis nor to the modern theory of representation or reflection; rather, it evokes the alchemist's notion of purification and of the transmutation of matter, in particular of metals.

Because of the dominant rational model of Western philosophy of sciences, alchemy is often taken to be a sort of charlatanry, a medieval pseudoscience, at best a precursor of modern scientific chemistry.[95] Mircea Eliade is one of the few who opposes this view. To consider alchemy a rudimentary form of chemistry is for him to reduce it to the level of a secular experimental science and to ignore its philosophical side, its sacred cosmology.[96] Alchemy should not be submitted to the same standard of validity as the other so-called positive sciences. It does not have, at least initially, the same function as chemistry. The ideal of the clearly delimited, "purified" object of modern science is not identical with the "purity" of spiritualized gold pursued by alchemy. Pure iron is a legitimate object of chemistry; for an alchemist it is still an imperfection of the world, and accepted by the poet only in a provocative way: *"je change l'or en fer/Et le paradis en enfer."*[97] Pure gold, or its demonic counterpart, symbolizes a mystic reunion of matter and spirit. Alchemical purification consists in a series of transmutations, metamorphoses, both within one realm and from one realm to another. Contrary to modern chemistry, alchemy purifies not so much through separation as through unification. To be sure, *separatio* is one of the traditional stages of alchemic process, but *coniunctio* or unification immediately follows it. The affirmation of the universal unity *(hen to pan)* of the "mercurial dragon of Greek alchemy" was echoed in the Middle Ages by the characterization of the *materia prima*—epitomized variously by quicksilver, sulfur, gold, fire, blood, lapis, spirit, sky, sea, mother, moon, chaos, etc.—as *Unica Res, Unum,* or Monad.[98] The famous Renaissance alchemist Hoghelande emphasizes this unitary character of the prime substance, and the unitary vision of the old masters of alchemy who "have compared the *prima materia* to everything, to male and female, hermaphroditic monster, to heaven and earth, to body and spirit, chaos, microcosm, and to the mixed mass *(massa confusa).*"[99] The universe born from this prime substance is unified, autonomous, and self-contained: "It contains in itself all colors and potentially all metals; there is nothing more wonderful in the world, for it begets itself, conceives itself and gives birth to itself."[100] It is the principle of metamorphosis that allows for this unity of the manifold within the world. The prevalent characteristic of alchemy, the one that makes it impossible to compare it with scientific chemistry, is thus its holistic vision. Modern sciences with their dominant technology owe their development and their competence precisely to the abandonment of the overall view of the world, to extreme specialization—an Aristotelian "purification" of their respective subjects. Alchemy on the other hand allows for the largest possible view of the universe. The language of purification is, nevertheless, retained. A Rosicrucian, Julius Sperber, for example, links this panoramic outlook to the procedure of alchemical purification in his *Isagoge de materia lapidis*:

> The philosophers' stone purifies and illuminates body and soul to such a degree that its possessor sees, as in a mirror, all celestial motions of constellations and of stellar influences from his solitary room without even seeing the firmament.[101]

This overall unity of matter and spirit governs C.G. Jung's own distinction between the practical chemical work in the laboratory and the psychic processes epitomized in the "various transformations of matter."[102] In this unitary perspective the practical effectiveness is less important than the realization of the overall "purificatory" movement of man and of the world. According to the recent students of alchemical texts, Michel Caron and Serge Hutin, "alchemy aims at the purification of Being; it strives to render man capable of acquiring the supreme knowledge."[103] The art of alchemy is often accompanied by ascetic exercises, which are also seen in cathartic terms: purification as a *conditio sine qua non* of knowledge. Thus a kind of "liberation," a delivery from "the blind forces of destiny," has to precede the famous alchemical Grand Work, which only then will lead to an effective "transmutation of the illusory into the real."[104] Rene Alleau, another contemporary representative of the alchemical tradition, emphasizes the role of cosmic analogy in the unification of Being and man. The masters of alchemy consider the *mineral Adam* to be the reflection of the Universe and of Man in the mirror of nature. Having mastered knowledge of the conditions governing the transformation of the *Metallic Microcosm*, man is able to discover and to understand analogically the rules of his/her proper metamorphoses. Purifying and making more perfect the *Subject of Wisdom*, capturing and absorbing energy which comes from other worlds, com-pressed by this mysterious *Magnet (Aimant)*, human being has the way of sowing the Light in the depth of his body and of his consciousness.[105]

Again, the notion of purification brings together human beings and the various realms of their activity. And again, the basic reality of the metallic (under)world points toward the original unity and the universal *telos* of gold. As a famous mythic alchemist puts it: "All metallic seed is the seed of gold: for gold is the intention of Nature with regard to all metals. If the base metals are not gold, it is only through some accidental hindrance: they are all potentially gold."[106] In order to succeed in the major task of the alchemical endeavor, however, an exceptional degree of purity is required. In Roger Bacon's words "it is according to the purity and impurity of the two aforesaid principles [*Argent-vive,* and *Sulphur*] that pure, and impure metals are engendered."[107] In the alchemical mode of thought, this transmutation should not be limited to metals. In the process of purification the mineral becomes organic and the organic spiritual. Thus the whole universe is to be in the state of a constant transformation. This is why Artaud writes also that "there is between the principle of the theater and that of alchemy a mysterious identity of essence."[108]

Artaud himself opposes alchemical thought and work to the scientific method of chemistry. The latter is for him only a "degenerated branch of Alchemy."[109] The method of chemistry is analytic, based on the gross separation of elements, and it corresponds to the *"éparpillement analytique des sentiments"* (analytic dispersal of sentiments) in the dominant theater of Artaud's day *(le théâtre habituel)*.[110] According to the alchemical idea of the theater, on the other hand, "the forms, the sentiments, the words, compose the image of a kind of living and synthetic whirl *(tourbillon vivant et synthétique),* in the midst of which the spectacle takes the aspect of a real transmutation" *(véritable transmutation)*.[111] The possibility of metamorphosis or transmutation, of crossing the boundaries of everyday reality, is what marks the alchemical or magical—which is also in Artaud's view the truly poetic—view of the world.

ANARCHIC POETICS

Artaud's parallel between classical theater and scientific chemistry on the one hand, and the theater of cruelty and alchemy on the other—a parallel that yields the polarity "analytic/synthetic"—might appear puzzling, and precisely from the point of view of his attitude toward the idea of order and anarchy. Both the *"éparpillement analytique"* (analytic dispersal)—the evils of chemistry and the traditional theater—and the tourbillon synthétique (synthetic whirl)—the principle of alchemy and of the theater of cruelty—evoke the idea of chaos and of anarchy. Indeed, the notion of anarchy is ambiguous in Artaud's writings. Sometimes it designates the decadent state of Western civilization and sometimes the essence of all poetry and in particular the essence of the theater of cruelty. In "No More Masterpieces," for example, Artaud blames our "spiritual anarchy and intellectual disorder" for the general anarchy of our age, leading to "boredom, inertia, and stupidity of everything."[112] On the other hand, in his "Alchemical Theater," Artaud proclaims anarchy the very principle of art: "It seems indeed that where simplicity and order reign, there can be no theater nor drama, and the true theater, like poetry as well, though by other means, is born out of a kind of anarchy that organizes itself *(d'une anarchie qui s'organise)* after philosophical battles which are the passionate aspect of these primitive unifications" *(de ces primitives unifications)*.[113] And in the spirit of Artaud's determination of poetry as originating from fire and anarchy, Roger Gilbert-Lecomte writes already in the year 1934: "When poetry is not somewhat anarchic, when it lacks fire and incandescence or the magnetic whirlwind of worlds in formation, it is not poetry."[114] It is the character of alchemical *initiation* that can explain this apparent inconsistency in Artaud's attitude toward anarchy and order. Such initiation consists of two principal stages. *First:* an extreme dissolution of the body: "It is necessary that the body (corpus) be initially dissolved, that the portals be opened, in order that nature could operate."[115] *Second:* an all-the-more-powerful reintegration and unification: "You will know that all mastery consists in dissolution followed by a coagulation."[116] The artistic principle Artaud has in mind is similar to this alchemical process; it can be called "con-fusion"—with a hyphen indicating the contradictory character of art:

> There is in all poetry an essential contradiction (contradiction essentielle). Poetry pulverized multiplicity *(multiplicité broyée)* and it produces flames. And poetry which restores order, first revives disorder, disorder with semblance ablaze; the multiple aspects of which are made to collide and are eventually brought to a single point: fire, gesture, blood, scream *(feu, geste, sang, cri)*.[117]

Heliogabalus, Roman emperor—the crowned anarchist—is for Artaud the model of an artist, practicing an accomplished poetry *(poésie réalisée)* as applied anarchy *(anarchie appliquée)*. Unleashing an endless chaos, he necessarily becomes its first victim, a victim "signaling through the flames."

In the theater *stricto sensu,* the theater of cruelty, the "synaesthetic" unity of art is not as readily apparent as in the classical poetics of the beautiful. It has this dangerous mark of anarchy, a conflicting, painful, and dissonant character analyzed by Burke, Kant, Lyotard, and others as the phenomenon of the sublime, the phenomenon poetically formulated by Rimbaud as the "disordering or deregulation of all the senses" *(déréglement des tous les sens)*.[118] Indeed, Artaud described the spectacle of the theater of cruelty as a "collision of objects, silences, shouts, and rhythms,"[119] and as a play of limitless *dissonances*.[120] The presence of huge puppet-monsters and other "plastic manifestations of forces" constitutes a true poetry "ready to disorganize and pulverize appearances according to the analogical, anarchistic principle of all genuine poetry."[121] But the spectacle of cruelty will recover the sense of "magical unification [. . .] in an atmosphere of hypnotic suggestion in which the mind is affected by a direct pressure upon the senses."[122]

Such an apparent "mix-up" of the various sensuous perceptions, like the blending and smelting of the elements in the alchemist's crucible, can lead to the unity of poetic experience only by transcending the categories of philosophical representation ("to analyze such a drama philosophically is impossible").[123] The final metamorphosis, the emergence of "spiritual gold," must remain a mystery, just as the successful alchemical transmutation remains a mystery. The work in the theater of cruelty should concentrate on the way toward the goal rather than on the goal itself, for "it follows from the very principle of alchemy not to let the spirit take its leap until it has passed through all the filters and foundations of existing matter, and to redouble this labor at the incandescent edges of the future" (*"dans les limbes incandescents de l'avenir"*).[124] And this labor of course never reaches its end. Such an alchemical way of proceeding recalls Plato's method of genuine philosophical "initiation," as described in the *Seventh Letter*, a method consisting of a long period of laborious study that might possibly result in a sudden flash: "like a fire kindled by a leaping spark."[125] Again the idea of chaos and confusion belongs to Artaud's aesthetics: it is a necessary principle of initiation (Greek *arkhê*) in the continuous process of metamorphosis and sublimation.

"CRUEL" METAPHYSICS

"By this double, I mean the great magic agent, of which the theater, in its forms, is only the figuration, waiting to become its transfiguration," writes Artaud, in a letter to Jean Paulhan.[126] It might appear paradoxical that Artaud himself appeals to Plato as a prophet of the cruel spectacle, which the philosopher foresaw in the Mysteries of Eleusis?[127] Perhaps not, if we remember that Plato's quarrel with the theater was caused mainly by the representational character of the latter and by the impossibility of distinguishing the genuine form of representation (*eikôn* or "image") from the spurious one (*eidôlon* or "simulacrum"), that is, by its necessarily misleading character. A spectacle of the theater of cruelty does not mask but, on the contrary, discloses the primordial sensuous and spiritual chaos to consciousness: "there is no cruelty without consciousness (*pas de cruauté sans conscience*)."[128] And the "true reality" is precisely that, which Aristotelian catharsis in all its interpretations has always tried to keep at bay, that is, the idea of the sublime indetermination (familial, religious, political) that might threaten the established order. The function of the cruel spectacle is to reveal this "underlying menace of a chaos as decisive as it is dangerous *(d'un chaos aussi décisif que dangereux)*."[129] A successful alchemical spectacle is neither a legitimate representation of a separate reality nor a mystifying deceit of a simulacrum. As to its ontological status, it is neither once nor twice removed from "the truth and the king." It is the event of truth as *alêtheia,* as concealment/unconcealment and eventually as mystery at the end of the process of a sublime transformation in the theater of cruelty.[130]

For Artaud, the best example, indeed the paradigm of sublimation and purity was the Eastern Balinese Theater, a performance of which he witnessed during the 1931 Colonial Exposition in Paris. He describes his impression of this performance in the famous essay "On the Balinese Theater," extolling all the elements of the spectacle, set, music, costumes, lights, and above all acting. The gestures of the actors in the Balinese Theater are, or at least appear to be, an effect of a long process of purification or sublimation. They seem to have lost any anchorage in immediate everyday reality and move to a spiritual realm of ritual. The abstraction and extreme generality of the situations is compensated by the "complex profusion of all the artifices of the stage" combined with the precision of a mathematical formula. This new "physical language based on signs rather than words"[131] constitutes in fact a "metaphysics of gesture." But "metaphysics" here is not opposed to the sensuous experience, to the "superabundance of impressions" emanating from the stage: "movements, forms, colors, vibrations, attitudes, cries,"[132] rather the latter is the only way of implementing the former. The complex movements of the actors that support the various impressions have to pass through the stage of dangerous turmoil that constantly threatens the equilibrium of this "metaphysics":

> Time and again you see them perform a kind of recovery with measured steps. Just as you think they are lost in an inextricable maze of measures, just as you feel them about to fall into confusion, they have a characteristic way of recovering their balance, a special way of propping up the body, the twisted legs, that gives the impression of a wet rag being wrung out in time—and in three final steps, which always lead inexorably toward the middle of the stage, the suspended rhythm is over and the beat resolved.[133]

The image of a wet rag *(un chiffon trop imprégné)* wrung out *(tordu)* and the recovering of balance in a centripetal movement of the actors evoke again the sublimating effect of the alchemist's melting pot. Such alchemical fusion and metamorphosis is also suggested by the music

> in which the most precious metals seem to be ground, in which springs of water seem to gush up as if in their natural state, and armies of insects march through vegetation, in which one seems to hear captured the very sound of light, in which the sound of deep solitudes seems to be reduced to flights of crystals, etc. etc.[134]

Thus *"meta-"* in Artaud's "metaphysics of gesture" should be understood as "with," "among," "together," and "along with," in addition to the obvious "after," and "beyond.' The "theater of cruelty" can be called "alchemical" because of its involvement in the process of *coniunctio* or "welding together" of various realms of experience into the total synaesthetic effect of spectacular purification or *sublimation*.

In the Balinese Theater, the master alchemist is not, as in the Western classical theater, the author but the director *(metteur en scène)* who becomes "a kind of magical conductor, a master of sacred ceremonies."[135] His task is not to express his "personal experience" but to reveal the "fabulous and obscure reality" repressed in everyday life. Indeed, the reality of the true theater, just like the reality of true alchemy, is *virtual*.[136] It does not refer to the surface of the human world: "[. . .] this reality is not human but inhuman, and man with his custom and his character counts for very little in it."[137] Both alchemy and the theater tend toward the absolutely pure state of the matter and of the spirit: "We are present at a mental alchemy which turns a state of mind into a gesture, the dry, bare, linear gesture that all our actions could have if they moved toward the absolute."[138] The latter is the absolute of sublimation.

Artaud's statement quoted above, concerning "the uselessness of the action" and the "purification" that would provoke and eventually protect against the danger of the cruel spectacle, should be understood in the light of these ideas of the virtual alchemical transformation. When attaining an extreme degree of cruelty, actions and gestures relinquish their human character and escape common measure.[139] Curnier thus formulates the end of the theater of cruelty: " *la revendication de la cruauté comme retour à la vérité de la condition d'existence et comme passage indispensable vers une recomposition de l'homme.*"[140] Poetry and the theater might be indeed able, through the extreme force born in the senses, to overcome everyday reality. Just as Plato's Socrates described the ideal realm,[141] Artaud describes the sensual realm: "[T]he images of poetry in the theater are a spiritual force that begins its trajectory in the senses and does without reality altogether."[142] As in the case of alchemical metamorphosis, the sublimation achieved by the theater of cruelty brings with it the suspension of the ordinary view of reality and the ordinary language that supports it, and eventually leads to the transformation of both.

Purification of language belongs to the tradition of Symbolist (theory of) poetry with its idea of alchemical or magic transformation. Indeed, the intended result of art, its *telos*, in Valéry's words, is the purity of language. The object and the power of such purifying transformation belong to the poetic word: "It should never be forgotten that the poetic form has been enlisted, down the ages, in the service of enchantment. Those who gave themselves up to the strange activities of magic must have believed in the power-of word."[143] The poetic power of word is to be distinguished from the rational force of *logos*. Not philosophical argument but magic incantation makes poetry powerful. Not logic, but the sensuous quality of the word is able to achieve transmutation. The primary auditory aspect of the word—its sonority—necessarily expands it in the direction of other senses. Yeats, using an explicitly alchemical terminology in extolling the transformative power of the word, points to the power of sight: "Solitary men in moments of contemplation receive, as I think, the creative impulse from the lowest of the nine Hierarchies, and so make and unmake mankind, and even the world itself, for does not 'the eye altering alter all'?"[144] The "altering eye" brings together the word and the world of the senses. Artaud's characterization of the language used in the theater of cruelty constitutes a perfect model of such integration:

[L]et there be the least return to the active, plastic, respiratory sources of language, let words be joined again to the physical motions that gave them birth, and let the discursive, logical aspect of speech disappear beneath its affective, physical side, i.e., let words be heard in their sonority rather than be exclusively taken for what they mean grammatically, let them be perceived as movements.[145]

This dynamic and sensuous character of language, the "vibratory action" of which should "exalt, benumb, charm, and arrest the sensibility,"[146] contains the transforming magic power of words as opposed to the representational character of language in the traditional Western theater: "[A]nd we want to restore to poetry its dynamic and virulent meaning, this magic potential of things. And thus conceive magic as releasing *(dégagement)* real energies, according to a precise ritual."[147] The "releasing" of energy should be understood here as a form of purification of any accidental violence that might evoke a representation of everyday reality.

In *The Theater and Its Double,* Artaud blames Aristotelian poetics because of its "analytic" separation between the realm of language *(logos* or *muthos)*[148] and reality *(ta erga),*[149] an analysis that is the condition of the "senseless" imitation or mimesis. In fact, Artaud is just as fervent an enemy of mimesis as Plato's Socrates in *The Republic.* But contrary to Brecht—who explicitly calls his theater "non-Aristotelian" and non-cathartic—it is not because of the cathartic identification but because of its detachment that Artaud rejects Aristotle's idea of theater. Whereas imitation corrupts the spectator by removing her/him from immediate contact with life, the *sublimation* or purification of the theater of cruelty will suppress the artificial distance of mimesis and bring the spectator into absolute proximity with the stage events, that is, with the pure manifestation of life. A literal, sensuous "identification" will thwart any endeavor to analyze and to appropriate them as representation through a verbal plot. If there is anything to be learned from such a spectacle, it is paradoxically the impossibility of learning—the uselessness of the action that, as mentioned above, cannot be performed again: "[T]he theater is the only place in the world where a gesture, once made, can never be made the same way twice."[150] This is, of course, paradoxical in view of the traditional theory of representation, in particular theatrical representation *(représentation* in French designates also—beside "representation"—a [repeatable] performance; "rehearsal" is called explicitly "répétition"). Magic and dreams provide models for such cruel immediacy of the spectacle.

The public will believe in the theater's dreams on condition that it take them for true dreams and not for a servile copy of reality; on condition that they allow the public to liberate within itself the magical liberties of dreams which it can only recognize when they are imprinted with terror and cruelty.[151]

Terror and cruelty, unlike the Aristotelian pity and fear, do not yield the balance between proximity and distance that could produce the effect of catharsis in the logical coherence of *muthos* or *logos*, and warrant the place of the representational theater within the poetics of the beautiful. Artaud's alchemical "purification" can only be understood in terms of the aesthetic of the sublime, as a challenge to the very principle of representation as separated from action.[152] The task of the cruel spectacle will be to render null and void the limits of classical theater: the separation *(khôrismos)* between the stage and the audience, between actors and characters, and between word and gesture. And this task of crossing the boundaries in the life-like uniqueness of the spectacle can be achieved through the magical transformation of sense, rather than through its verbal metaphorization.

With all its emphasis on sensuality, Artaud's aesthetics of cruelty seems to escape the pitfalls of modern aestheticism. The extreme passion invested in all Artaud's writings, as well as in the figures of his characters, excludes any notion of a detached aesthetic satisfaction. In the theater, as Artaud imagines it, the purity of extreme gestures (*les gestes les plus extrêmes*) will be achieved through Artaud's *mise en scène* of his own plays but also of the texts that, within the tradition, resisted the pressure of the Aristotelian catharsis. The poet, in Artaud's view, is neither aesthete "dallying with forms" nor even author, but martyr "like victims burnt at the stake, signaling through the flames" *(comme des suppliciés que l'on brûle et qui font des signes sur leurs bûchers)*.[153] His gesture is precisely that—a gesture in the strong sense given to it by Varro and more recently by Agamben:[154] an event of suffering, supporting (*gerere,* as opposed to both *facere* and *agere*) the transformability of matter and spirit, exhibiting the pure potentiality of gold rather than gold itself.[155]

Thus the conception of "fiery purification" in Artaud's theater of cruelty—of the happening of cruelty as pure gesture of unrestrained passion—opposes both the classical notion of representation or mimesis and the modern notion of distanced aesthetic enjoyment. In fact, the theater of cruelty is not theater, and the aesthetics of cruelty is not aesthetics in the ordinary modern sense given to these notions. The extreme cruelty and its purification—"fiery," "alchemical," "magical"—should be understood in terms of the sublime metamorphosis as that which transcends the limits of aesthetic representation.

Artaud does not accept the spirit/matter dichotomy. There is a unity of the two, especially in art: "Matter exists only *through* the spirit, and the spirit only *in* matter. But at the end of the day, it's always the spirit which retains supremacy."[156] This is the principle on which Artaud's culture-in-action is based. Spirit retains supremacy, but only in association with matter, as he says in *Heliogabalus*. Metaphysical ideas, such as idea of chaos, anarchy, and revolt can only act through matter. They need the violence of thought or cruelty: "In our present state of degeneration, it is through the skin that metaphysics must be made to re-enter our minds" (*dans l'etat de dégénérescence où nous sommes, c'est par la peau qu'on fera rentrer la métaphysique dans les esprits*).[157] Artaud calls such active thought "culture-in-action." Cruelty is the name of its "anarchic" principle.

NOTES

1. Derrida, *Writing and Difference*, 249; In "Le théâtre de la cruauté et la clôture de la représentation," 366: *Artaud s'est tenu au plus proche de la limite: la possibilité et l'impossibilité du théâtre pur.*

2. Artaud, *The Theater and its Double*, 7 [henceforth *ThD*]; "Le théâtre et son double," in *Œuvres Complètes*, vol. IV, 9 [henceforth *ŒC*]: *Le plus urgent ne me paraît pas tant de défendre une culture dont l'existence n'a jamais sauvé un homme du souci de mieux vivre et d'avoir faim, que d'extraire de ce que l'on appelle la culture, des idées dont la force vivante est identique à celle de la faim.*

3. Derrida, *L'écriture et la différence*, 343. *Writing and Difference*, 234: "The Theater of cruelty is not a *representation*. It is life itself, in the extent to which life is unpresentable. Life is the nonrepresentable origin of representation. 'I have therefore said "cruelty" as I might have said "life".'" See Artaud, *Letter à Jean Poulain* de 9 novembre 1932 in *ŒC* IV, 110; *ThD*, 114.

4. *ThD*, 7; *ŒC* IV, 9.

5. *ThD*, 9; *ŒC* IV, 11: *nous sentons une odeur blanche, blanche comme on peut parler d'un "mal blanc." Comme le fer rougi à blanc on peut dire que tout ce qui est excessif est blanc; et pour un Asiatique la couleur blanche est devenue l'insigne de la plus extrême décomposition.*

6. *ThD*, 11; *ŒC* IV, 13: *A notre idée inerte et désintéressée de l'art une culture authentique oppose une idée magique et violamment égoïste, c'est-à-dire intéressée.*

7. Deleuze, *Difference and Repetition*, 28.

8. Ibid., 29. *Différence et répétition*, 44: *la cruauté, c'est. seulement LA détermination, ce point précis où le déterminé entretient son rapport essentiel avec l'indéterminé, cette ligne rigoureuse abstraite qui s'alimente au clair-obscur.*

9. *ThD*, 7–8; *ŒC* IV, 9–10: (translation modified); *sytèmes à penser ...; leur nombre et leur contradictions caractérisent notre vieille culture européenne et française: mais où voit-on que la vie, notre vie, ait jamais été affectée par ces systèmes.*

10. Blanchot, *The Book to Come*, 3; *Le livre à venir* 9: *l'inhumanité de tout chant humain*.
11. Homer, *Odyssey* XII, 39ff.
12. Aristotle, *Poetics* 1449 b 27–8.
13. Ibid. 1452 b 30ff; cf. Else, *Aristotle's Poetics*, 423–47.
14. Ibid. 1453 b 8–13.
15. Althusser "On Brecht and Marx," 145.
16. This view of "Aristotle's coercive system of tragedy" has been developed by Boal in his *Theater of the Oppressed*, chapter 1.
17. See Girard, *La Violence et le sacré* (1972); *Violence and the Sacred*, and Turner, *From Ritual to Theater: The Human Seriousness of Play*.
18. Theater is *"philosophoterôn historias"* (more philosophical than history), according to Aristotle, *Poetics*, 1451b5–6; although he speaks of poetry in general, the immediately following remarks refer explicitly to comedy and tragedy.
19. Artaud, *ThD*, 102; *ŒC* IV, 98.
20. Artaud, *Selected Writings*, 303 (translation modified); *"Il ne s'agit pas de sortir à tout instant sur la scène le couteau du boucher, mais de réintroduire dans chaque geste de théâtre la notion d'une sorte de cruauté cosmique sans laquelle il n'y aurait ni vie, ni réalité."*Artaud's letter to Jean Paulhan from 12 of September 1932 in *ŒC* V, 110.
21. p. 19f. Farther on Tonelli writes in *L'Esthétique de la cruauté* that "with reference to the Aristotelian conception, one should not say catharsis, but rather anti-catharsis" 47, but he does not develop this idea and do not abandon the traditional terminology.
22. Artaud, *ThD*, 90; *ŒC* IV, 87.
23. Artaud, *ThD*, 82f; *ŒC* IV, 85.
24. Artaud, *ThD*, 13; *ŒC* IV, 14.
25. Artaud, *ThD*, 116; *ŒC* IV, 112: *balaye l'individualité humaine*.
26. Artaud, *ThD*, 15ff; *ŒC* IV, 15ff.
27. Artaud, *ThD*, 24; *ŒC* IV, 23.
28. Artaud, *ThD*, 79; *ŒC* IV, 77.
29. Artaud, *ThD*, 32; *ŒC* IV, 31.
30. Artaud, *ThD*, 27; *ŒC* IV, 26–7.
31. Artaud, *ThD*, 30; *ŒC* IV, 29.
32. Artaud, *ThD*, 101; *ŒC* IV, 98.
33. Artaud, *ThD*, 102; *ŒC* IV, 98.
34. Artaud, *ThD*, 103; *ŒC* IV, 99.
35. The title of drama by John Ford *Tis Pity She's a Whore* in Maeterlinck's translation.
36. Artaud, *ThD*, 29; *ŒC* IV, 28.
37. Artaud, *The Cenci*, Act IV, scene III in fine.
38. Artaud, *ThD*, 67; *ŒC* IV, 64.
39. Artaud, *Heliogabalus*, 50; *Héliogabale*, 425.
40. Artaud, *Heliogabalus*, 49; *Héliogabale*, 425.
41. Artaud, *ThD*, 43; *ŒC* IV, 41.

42. Plato, *Republic*, 377ab, 379a, 395c-d, 398b, 400d-402d, and *passim*.
43. See Barish, *The Antitheatrical Prejudice*.
44. The consecrated English phrase "idea of chaos," if not strictly equivalent to the French *"idée sur le chaos,"* is certainly evocative; it is not inappropriate, in view of the explicit reference to Plato's *Ideas* in the same essay. See Artaud, *"La Mise en scène et la Métaphysique,"* in *ŒC* IV, 35; "Metaphysics and the Mise en Scène," in *ThD*, 36.
45. *ŒC* IV, 43; *ThD*, 44.
46. *ŒC* IV, 10; *ThD*, 8.
47. Boal in his *Teatro de Oprimido*; *Theater of the Oppressed*, 122; cf. Birringer, *Theater, Theory, Postmodernism*, 146–68.
48. Aristotle, *Poetics*, 1448b9–12.
49. Aristotle, *Poetics*, chapter XV; in his famous speech of Shakespeare's *Troilus and Cressida* (act I.scene III, 75ff.), (The Riverside ed.) 455, Ulysses calls these distinctions "degrees" and deplores the anarchy caused by their loss.
50. Aristotle, *Poetics*, 1450b17–20; cf. Artaud *ThD*, 117–18.
51. *ŒC* IV, 114; *ThD*, 117f.
52. Not "just . . . as great" as the English translation has it.
53. *Logos* is identified with *muthos* by Aristotle, e.g. *Poetics*, 1454b35, 1455a17.
54. "We can perfectly well continue to conceive of a theater based upon the authority of the text *(la prépondérance du texte)* more and more wordy, diffuse, and boring, to which the aesthetics of the stage would be subject. But this conception of the theater . . . is ... certainly its perversion" (*ŒC*. IV, 102; *ThD*, 106).
55. *ŒC* IV, 115; *ThD*, 118.
56. *ŒC* IV, 116; *ThD*, 119.
57. *ŒC* IV, 91; *ThD*, 94.
58. *ŒC* IV, 88; *ThD*, 91.
59. Letter to Roger Blin from 25 March 1946 in *ŒC* XI (Paris: Gallimard, 1974), 215.
60. *ŒC* IV, 79; *ThD*, 81; cf. Grotowski, "Il n'était pas entièrement lui-même," 1888.
61. *ŒC* IV, 84; *ThD*, 86; cf. 93 and 96, respectively.
62. *ŒC* IV, 71; *ThD*, 73.
63. *ŒC* IV, 114; *ThD*, 116.
64. *ŒC* IV, 64; *ThD*, 67.
65. *ŒC* IV, 121; *ThD*, 124.
66. de Rotrou, *Le Véritable Saint Genest*.
67. *ŒC* IV, 27–30; *ThD*, 28–30; *ŒC* IV, 147–210; *ŒC*. VII, 9–137.
68. Aristotle, *Poetics*, 15, 1454a.
69. Artaud, *Heliogabalus*, 126; *Héliogabale*, 466.
70. See, e.g., Artaud's letter to Jean Paulhan from 25 January 1936, in *ŒC* V, 272f.
71. The latter interpretation might be suggested by the standard translation of the French *"sublimation"* by "purification."
72. J. Lear, "Katharsis," in Oksenberg Rorty (ed.), *Aristotle's Poetics*, 334f.

73. *ŒC* IV, 77; *ThD.*, 79, Artaud's emphasis.

74. *ŒC* IV, 110; *ThD*, 114; cf. *ŒC* IV, 99; *ThD*, 103: "It seems to me that creation and life itself are defined only by a kind of rigor, hence a fundamental cruelty, which leads things to their ineluctable end at whatever cost."

75. *ŒC* IV, 110; *ThD*, 114.

76. *ŒC* IV, 98; *ThD*, 102.

77. "*Quels que soient les conflicts qui hantent la tête d'une époque, je défie bien un spectateur à qui les scènes violentes auront passé leur sang, qui aura senti en lui le passage d'une action supérieure, qui aura vu un éclair dans les faits extraordinaires et essentiels de sa pensée—la violence et le sang ayant été mis au service de la* violence de la pensée—*je le défie de se livrer au dehors à des idées de guerre, d'émeute et d'assassinat hasardeux*" (*ŒC* IV, 80; *ThD*, 82; my emphasis).

78. Girard, *Violence and the Sacred*, 49ff.; cf. Oksenberg Rorty *Aristotle's Poetics*, 2f.

79. Shakespeare, *Troilus and Cressida*, act I, scene III.

80. The analysis and critique of the semantic cluster of the "propre" belongs to Derrida's deconstruction of Western metaphysics; see, e.g., J. Derrida, "Le théâtre de la cruauté et la cloture de la *représentation*" in *L'écriture et la différence*; "The Theater of Cruelty and the Closure of Representation," in *Writing and Difference*, and "La Mythologie blanche: La métaphore dans le texte philosophique" in *Marges de la philosophie*; "White Mythology: Metaphor in the Text of Philosophy" in *Margins of Philosophy*.

81. In *Platonis Opera*, ed. John Burnet (1903, reprint, Oxford: Oxford University Press, 1984), 66b–67b: pure being, pure knowledge. English translation consulted: Plato, *Phaedo*, in *Complete Works*; numbers and letters conform to the Stephanus pagination, adopted by most translators; where not specified translations are mine.

82. Plato, *Phaedo*, 81a.

83. Plato, *The Republic*, 399e.

84. Or, in Shakespeare's *Midsummer Night's Dream*, a weaver playing Pyramus, or Thisbe, or a lion.

85. Plato, *The Republic*, 414–15.

86. See St. Augustine, *The City of God, Against the Pagans*, vol. I, book xxxiii, 132–5; cf. Artaud, "Le Théâtre et la Peste" *ŒC* vol. IV, 25. Artaud, *ThD*, 26; cf. Barish, *The Antitheatrical Prejudice*, 60.

87. See, e.g., Else, *Plato and Aristotle on Poetry*, p. 69: "It has always been acknowledged, in principle, that the *Poetics* is a reply to Plato's attacks on poetry."

88. See, e.g., Aristotle, *Poetics*, 1454a16–36.

89. Slavery, for example, and inequality of genders are said to be natural in Aristotle's *Politics*, 1254b13–55a3.

90. See Perloff, *The Poetics of Indeterminacy*, 4; Paul Valéry's writings (for example "Poésie et pensée abstraite" in *Œuvres* vol. I, 1314 ff.) testify most clearly to the subsistence of the Cartesian ideal in modern poetics.

91. Some interpreters, although pointing to the specificity of Artaud's "theory of catharsis," eventually assimilate it to the Aristotelian tradition; Sellin for example writes: "Artaud's concepts to some extent repeat those of Aristotle, but if the ultimate

intent is the same, namely catharsis, the means by which Artaud thought catharsis might be achieved differs on several major points from that of Aristotle ... The fundamental differences between the two theories may be attributable in part to the passage of time ..." 96 and 99; cf. Tonelli, *L'esthétique de la cruauté.*, 42–8; Greene, on the other hand, inscribes Artaud's work in the general movement of Surrealism, preoccupied with the purification of language, see her *Antonin Artaud: Poet without Words*, 104ff.

92. Artaud, *ŒC* IV, 80; *ThD*. 82.

93. Artaud, *ŒC* IV, 80; Helen Weaver translates more literally—actually transliterates—the French *sublimation* by the English "sublimation"—*Antonin Artaud, Selected Writings*, [henceforth *Selected Writings*], 259.

94. Artaud, *ŒC* IV, 80; *ThD*, 82.

95. The word "chemistry" comes from "alchemy," the etymology of which is uncertain, but it certainly has its roots in the domain of metallurgy: *khemein*, an Egyptian word meaning "the preparation of the black ore or powder," or *kheuma*, a Greek word for "smelting," "casting"—see Franklyn, *A Survey of the Occult*, 2 and Knapp, *Theater and Alchemy*, 4.

96. Eliade, *Forgerons et Alchimistes*, 9–11; cf. Bachelard, *La formation de l'esprit scientifique*, 46f.

97. "I change gold into iron/and paradise into hell"—Baudelaire, "L'alchimie de la douleur," in *Oeuvres Completes*, 73.

98. Jung, "Psychologie und Alchemie," Vol. 12, 365–7; "Psychology and Alchemy" in *The Collected Works*. Vol. 12, 306.

99. Hoghelande, *Liber de alchemiae dfficultatibus*, 178f., quoted by C.G. Jung, ibid.

100. Ibid.

101. Sperber, *Isagoge de materia lapidis*, quoted by Caron and Serge Rutin in *Les Alchimistes*, 163.

102. Jung, op. cit., 258.

103. Caron and Rutin, *Les Alchemistes*, 95f.

104. Ibid.

105. Alleau, *Aspects de L'alchimie traditionnelle*, 143–4.

106. Eirenaeus Philaletes, an alchemist of the 16th century cited in Franklyn, *A Survey of the Occult*, 5.

107. Bacon, *The Mirror of Alchimy*, 4. Cf. Ambelain, *L'Alcaimie spirituelle*, 52.

108. (my translation); *ŒC* IV, 46: *Il y a entre le principe du théâtre et celui de l'alchimie une mystérieuse identité d'essence.*

109. Artaud, "Lettre à *Comoedia*" (September 18, 1932), in *ŒC* V, 33.

110. Ibid.

111. Ibid.

112. Artaud, *ŒC* IV, 77 and 81; *ThD*, 79 and 83.

113. Artaud, *ŒC* IV, 49; *ThD*, 51.

114. Artaud, *ŒC* II, 245: *"et quand elle [poésie] n'est pas si peu que ce soit anarchique, quand il n'y a pas dans un poème le degré du feu et de l'incandescence, et ce tourbillonnement magnétique des mondes en formation, ce n'est pas la poésie."*

115. Sethon, the Cosmopolitan, *"Novum lumen chymicum de lapide Philosopharum,"* quoted in R. Ambelain, *Alchimie spirituelle*, 52.
116. Grand, *Le Livre des huit chapitres*, 53.
117. Artaud, *Heliogabalus*, 103; *Héliogabale*, 453 in Œuvres [2004] (translation modified).
118. Rimbaud, "Letter to Paul Demeny" in *Poésies, Une saison en enfer. Illuminations*, 202–3; *"Le Poète se fait* voyant *par un long, immense et raisonné* déréglement *de* tousles sens. *Toutes les formes d'amour, de souffrance, de folie; il cherche lui même, il épuise en lui tousles poisons, pour n'en garder que les quintessences. Ineffable torture, où il a besoin de toute la foi, de toute la force surhumaine, où il devient entre tous le grand malade, le grand criminel, le grand maudit,—et le suprême Savant!";* see also *Œvres* (Paris: Classiques Garnier, 2000), 364–5, and the note of Suzanne Bernard and Andre Guyaux on the double (anarchic and demiurgic) aspect of Rimbaud's poetics.
119. Artaud, *ŒC* IV, 120; *ThD,* 124.
120. Artaud, *EC* IV, 109; *ThD,* 113: "The secret of theater in space is dissonance, dispersion of timbres, and the dialectic discontinuity of expression"
121. Artaud, *ŒC* IV 121; *ThD,* 125.
122. Artaud, *ŒC* IV 121; *ThD,* 125.
123. Artaud, *CEC* IV, 48; *ThD,* 50.
124. Artaud, *CEC* IV, 49; *ThD,* 51.
125. Plato, *Seventh Letter,* 341d; Deleuze compares the Platonic method of dialectical division to the search for gold: *"La recherche de l'or, voilà le modèle de la division"*—Deleuze, *Différence et répétition*, 84; *Difference and Repetition,* 60.
126. Letter from 25 January 1936 (my translation); Artaud, *ŒC* V, 272f: *[P]ar ce double j'entends le grand agent magique dont le théâtre par ses formes n'est que la figuration, en attendant qu'il en devienne la transfiguration.*
127. Artaud, *ŒC* IV, 50; *ThD,* 52.
128. Artaud, *ŒC* IV, 98; *ThD,* 102.
129. Artaud, *ŒC* IV, 48; *ThD,* 51; cf. Artaud, *ŒC* IV, 77; *ThD,* 79: "We are not free. And the sky can still fall on our heads. And the theater has been created in order to teach us that first of all."
130. It is this view of theater that functions as a model for Deleuze's "philosophy of difference"—see Deleuze, *Différence et répétition*, 17; *Difference and Repetition,* 8; cf. Foucault, "Theatrum Philosophicum" 902ff. and Puchner, "The Theater in Modernist Thought," 523ff.
131. Artaud, *ŒC* IV, 52; *Selected Writings,* 215.
132. Artaud, *ŒC* IV, 54; *Selected Writings,* 217.
133. Artaud, *ŒC* IV, 55–6; *Selected Writings,* 219.
134. Artaud, *ŒC* IV, 56; *Selected Writings,* 219.
135. Artaud, *ŒC* IV, 57; *Selected Writings,* 220f.
136. Artaud, *ŒC* IV, 46; *ThD,* 48: "It is that alchemy and the theater are so to speak virtual arts, and do not carry their end—or their reality—within themselves."
137. Artaud, *ŒC* IV, 46; *ThD,* 48.
138. Artaud, *ŒC* IV, 64; *Selected Writings,* 226.

139. See Agamben, "Note on Gesture" in *Means without End*, 49ff.

140. Curnier, *A Vif*, 25. "The revindication of cruelty as the return to the truth of the condition of existence and as indispensable passage towards recompositing man." (my translation).

141. Plato, The Republic, Book VII.

142. Artaud, *ŒC* IV, 24; *ThD*, 25.

143. Valéry, *Variété II*, 156; cf. Zabriskie-Temple, *The Critic's Alchemy*, 14.

144. Yeats, *Selected Criticism*, 48.

145. Artaud, *ŒC* IV, 115–16; *ThD*, 119.

146. Artaud, *ŒC* IV, 86 and 88; *ThD*, 89 and 91.

147. Artaud, *ŒC* IV, 217; my translation.

148. *Logos* is identified with *muthos* in Aristotle's *Poetics*, e.g. 1454b35, 1455a17.

149. See Aristotle, *Poetics*, 1448b9–12.

150. Artaud, *ThD*, 75; *ŒC* IV, p. 73: *Le théâtre est le seul endroit au monde où un geste fait ne se recommence pas deux fois.*

151. Artaud, *ŒC*, IV, 83–4; *ThD*, 86.

152. Cf. Borie, *Antonin Artaud: le theatre et le retour aux sources*, 126.

153. Artaud, *ŒC* IV, 14; *ThD*, 13.

154. Varro, *On the Latin Language*, VI, VIII 77, 245, in Agamben, *Means without End*, 56–7.

155. As to the image of death as supreme purification, see Artaud, *ŒC I*, 204; and "L'éperon malicieux, le double-cheval" in Botteghe Oscure, No.8, 1951, 11; cf. Green, op. cit., 111.

156. Artaud, *Heligabalus*, 65; *Héligabale* 433: *La matière n'existe que par l'esprit, et l'esprit que dans la matière. Mais en fin de compte, c'est toujour l'esprit qui conserve la suprématie.*

157. Artaud, *ŒC* IV, 95; The *ThD*, 99.

Conclusion

The phenomena and the concepts of culture and cruelty, but also those of nihilism and purification turned out to be ambiguous, and this is what makes their analysis difficult. But perhaps in this ambiguity lies also their force. They appear (phenomena and concepts) to explode the system of binary oppositions in which they are situated. The words culture and cruelty are ambiguous not only in themselves, but especially they are in ambiguous relation to each other. They are dependent on each other, they condition, and limit each other.

Cruelty is the ultimate opposition to culture. At the simple level, cruelty can function as a vaccination does, can prevent much cruelty by intensively representing its small part. Artaud perhaps best formulates this thought, but the same idea we find in Nietzsche and Dostoevsky:

> Whatever the conflicts that haunt the mind of a given period, I defy any spectator to whom such violent scenes will have transferred their blood, who will have felt in himself the transit of a superior action, who will have seen extraordinary and essential movements of his thought illuminated in extraordinary deeds—the violence and blood having been placed at the service of the *violence of the thought*—I defy that spectator to give himself up, once outside the theater, to ideas of war, riot, and blatant murder.[1]

Cruelty thus can show that what is inacceptable in our otherwise accepted culture, in other words, that what would provoke our feeling of shame or, at least feeling of uneasiness, really exists and should be shown as such.

Culture can be protective of the boundaries of decency but can also oppress as ideology and propaganda, give rise to nihilism. Nihilism itself could be ambiguous, secure the cultural status quo, and also bring the fall of the corrupted culture. In this case, nihilism is the symptom of the degeneracy of culture. Cruelty, which is the ultimate negation of culture, could also mark its regeneration. In fact, cruelty opposes the extreme nihilism, the passive nihilism, in the form of indifference. Cruelty in disclosing its vicious side manifests at the same time its original vitality. It forces the nihilist to look deep in his/her protective barriers and to see beyond them. Purification is a special case of ambiguity, it can be used as a means of re-establishing the binary oppositions and, as shown by Dostoevsky, Nietzsche, and Artaud, breaking all boundaries.

It is mainly in the realm of art that such attempt, such dangerous experience is possible. Art is "a counter-movement to nihilism," writes Nietzsche, but all of our authors could sign the confirmation of it. Art is something "to get us out of our marasmus, of boredom, inertia, and stupidity of everything." Artaud diagnoses here the main evil of our culture. It is nihilism, indifference to everything, desire to theorize everything, to think abstractly. As Nietzsche, Dostoevsky, and Camus have shown, this trend gives rise to the emptiness of heart, contempt of feelings, as in the case of the underground man, in Dostoevsky, or last men or good men in Nietzsche. There is no use to deny the advantages of reason, but feeling needs to associate with them. "Feeling of thought" (*chuvstvo mysli*), or "violence of thought" (*la violence de la pensée*) union of two apparently contradictory notions could perhaps constitute the solution to this dilemma. "There is no language for the feeling," claimed D. H. Lawrence. Perhaps the so-called "feeling of thought" is the answer to this problem. Perhaps, it is cruelty or gut feeling that should complete thought by allowing to distinguish between two aspects of ambiguous terms and phenomena. The experience (*experiri*, or the feeling of danger) should be the condition of our decisions. The hero and narrator of Vonnegut's novel *Slaughterhouse 5* expresses this best: "Those who approved it [massacre of Dresden] were neither wicked nor cruel, though it may well be that they were too remote from the harsh realities of war to understand fully the appalling destructive power of air bombardment in the spring of 1945."[2] "Too remote" is Vonnegut's expression of indifferent attitude, focusing on plans of bombardment and abstract numbers of casualties. Even the events of Auschwitz are mainly seen in terms of numbers, and not the experience, be it literary, of the massacre. We do not want to dwell on the events of Holocaust; Wiesel's original title of *Night* was *And the World Remained Silent*, that is indifferent, which was the expression not only of the end solution, with the whole Western world watching, and refraining from action, but also of experiencing difficulties of publishing his manuscript in Yiddish; nobody was interested.

Our time is exceptionally rich in massacres but at the same time we are unable to face them. We can see cruelty only from a distance. Culture of nihilism and technoscience is a self-satisfied state of security and cowardice like, for example, "fighting" with bomb airplanes and drones, which remove the "fighters" from the battlefield, and place them in secure conditions. There is no more physical contact with an adversary, whose bodies and those of their families are exposed to the actions of the cowardly agents/officials of death. The economic development and moral decadence forces us to use bodies of animals as well, to satisfy our culinary and vestmental "needs." Admittedly, it was always thus, but slaughter was never remote. Today, on the contrary, the culture of technoscience results in cultural development or rather moral recession and tries not to see blood, not be associated with killing.

Recent discussion around the clip of the band Rammstein for the song *Deutschland* has shown that the artistic principle of cruelty is not easily accepted in our culture. The song and the clip, in a Nietzschean way, show the history of Germany from the wars of the Gotts to the Holocaust. The main point of the debate consisted in the question: could the cruelty of the Holocaust be represented? Could the cruel images be used as art? The answer should be yes. The function of art is precisely to question the nihilism of indifference. The opponents of this clip would rather not be disturbed by cruel images and live quietly, visiting the monuments, museums, and lamenting the number of victims. Art, on the contrary should disturb and question.[3]

It is this indifference that cruelty tends to reveal and make people participate in the slaughter, or else refrain from it, not send rockets unless they are able to imagine their children under the ruins.

NOTES

1. *ThD*, 82; *ŒC* IV, 80; (my emphasis): *Quels que soient les conflits qui hantent la tête d'une époque, je défie bien un spectateur à qui les scènes violentes auront passé leur sang, qui aura senti en lui le passage d'une action supérieure, qui aura vu un éclair dans les faits extraordinaires et essentiels de sa pensée–la violence et le sang ayant été mis au service de la* violence de la pensée–je le défie de se livrer au dehors à des idées de guerre, d'émeute et d'assassinat hasardeux.

2. Vonnegut, *Slaughterhouse 5*, 240.

3. https://www.youtube.com/watch?v=NeQM1c-XCDc, and https://www.blo omberg.com/opinion/articles/2019-04-02/rammstein-rock-video-sparks-debate-o ver-german-national-identity.

Bibliography

Adelman, Gary. *Retelling Dostoevsky: Literary Responses and Other Observations.* London: Associated University Press, 2001.
Agamben, Giorgio. *Means without End: Notes on Politics.* Translated by Vincenzo Binetti and Cesare Casarino. Minneapolis: University of Minnesota Press, 2000.
———. *Mezzi senza fine: Note sulla politica.* Torino: Bollati Boringhieri, 1996.
———. *Quel che resta di Auschwitz: L'archivio e il testimone.* Torino: Bollati Boringhieri, 1998.
———. *Remnants of Auschwitz: The Witness and the Archive.* Translated by Daniel Heller-Roazen. New York: Zone Books, 1999.
Ahern, Daniel R. *Nietzsche as Cultural Physician.* University Park: The Pennsylvania State University Press, 1995.
Albrecht, Thomas *The Medusa Effect.* Albany: State University of New York Press, 2009.
Alejandro, Roberto. *Nietzsche and the Drama of Historiography.* Notre Dame, IN: University of Notre Dame Press, 2011.
Alleau, René. *Aspects de L'alchimie traditionnelle.* Paris: Editions de Minuit, 1953.
Allison, David B. *The New Nietzsche: Contemporary Styles of Interpretation.* Cambridge, MA: The MIT Press (1985), 1997.
———. *Reading the New Nietzsche.* Lanham, NY: Rowman & Littlefield Publishers, INC, 2001.
Althusser, Louis. "On Brecht and Marx," in *Louis Althusser.* Edited by Warren Montag. Translated by Max Statkiewicz. New York: Palgrave MacMillan, 2003.
Ambelain, Robert. *L'Alchimie spirituelle: La voie intérieure.* Paris: La Diffusion Scientifique, 1974.
Arendt, Dieter. *Nihilismus; Die Anfänge von Jacobi bis Nietzsche.* Köln: Verlag Jakob Hegner, 1970.
Aristotle. *De Arte Poetica Liber.* Edited by Rudolfus Kassel. Oxford: Oxford University Press, 1965.

———. *Metaphysics*. Greek text with English translation by High Tredennick (1936), Cambridge MA: Harvard University Press, 1989.

———. *The Poetics*. Greek text with English translation by Stephen Halliwell. Cambridge, MA: Harvard University Press, 1995.

———. *Politics*. Greek text with English translation by H. Rackham (1932). Cambridge MA: Harvard University Press, 1977.

Arnold, Matthew. *Culture and Anarchy*. Edited by Samuel Lipman. New Haven: Yale University Press, 1994.

Artaud, Antonin. *Antonin Artaud Selected Writings*. Edited by Susan Sontag. NewYork: Farrar, Straus and Giroux, 1976.

———. *The Cenci*. Translated by Simon Watson Taylor. New York: Grove Press, Evergreen, 1970.

———. *Œuvres Complètes*, vol. V, Paris: Gallimard, 1979.

———. *Héliogabale ou l'Anarchiste couronné*, in *Œuvres Complètes*, vol. VII, Paris: Gallimard, 1978.

———. *Heliogabalus or, the Crowned Anarchist*. Translated by Alexis Lykiard. Solar Books, 2004.

———. *Le théâtre et son double* [1938] in *Œuvres Complètes*, vol. IV, Paris: Gallimard, 1978.

———. *Les Cenci*, in *Œuvres Complètes*, vol. IV, Paris: Gallimard, 1978.

———. *The Theater and Its Double*. Translated by Mary Caroline Richards. New York: Grove Weidenfeld, 1958. Augustine, St. *The City of God, Against the Pagans*. Translated by George E. McCracken (1957). Cambridge, MA: Harvard University Press, 1966.

Babich, Babette E. "*Mousikē Technē*: The Philosophical Practice of Music in Plato. Nietzsche, and Heidegger," in *Between Philosophy and Poetry. Writing, Rhythm, History*. Edited by Verdicchio, Massimo and Robert Burch. New York: Continuum, 2002.

———. *Words in Blood, Like Flowers. Philosophy and Poetry, Music and Eros in Hölderlin, Nietzsche, and Heidegger*. Albany: State University of New York Press, 2006.

Bachelard, Gaston. *La formation de l'esprit scientifique*. 7th ed. Paris: Vrin, 1970.

Bacon, Roger. *The Mirror of Alchimy*. Edited by Stanton J. Linden (rep.) New York and London: Garland Publishing, Inc., 1597.

Bakhtin, Mikhail. *Вопросы Литературы и Эстетики*. Москва: Художественная литература, 1975.

———. *Проблемы Творчества/Проблемы Поэтики Достоевского*. 1929, 1963; Киев: NEXT, 1994.

———. "The Problem of Content, Material, and Form in Verbal Act (1924)." Translated by Kenneth Brostrom, in *Art and Answerability. Early Philosophical Essays*. Edited by Michael Holquist and Vadim Liapunov. Austin: University of Texas Press, 1990.

———. *Problems of Dostoevsky's Poetics*. Translated by Caryl Emerson. Minneapolis: The University of Minnesota Press, 1984.

Barish, Jonas. *The Antitheatrical Prejudice*. Berkley: University of California Press, 1981.

Baudelaire, Charles. *Oeuvres Completes*. Edited by Claude Pichois. Paris: Gallimard: Bibliothèque de la Pleiade, 1961.
Baudrillard, Jean. *Fatal Strategies* Translated by Philippe Beitchman and W. G. J. Niesluchowski. Los Angeles CA: Semiotext(e), 1990.
———. *Les Stratégies fatales*. Paris: Grasset, 1983.
Beardsworth, Richard. "Nietzsche, Nihilism and Spirit," in *Nihilism Now. Monsters of Energy*. Edited by Keith Ansell Pearson and Diane Morgan. New York: St. Martin's Press, 2000.
Beauvoir, Simone de. *The Ethics of Ambiguity*. Translated by Bernard Frechtman. New York: Citadel Press (1948), 1976.
———. *Pour une morale de l'ambiguïte*. Paris: Gallimard, 1947.
Benjamin, Walter. "The Destructive Character," in *Reflections: Essays, Aphorisms, Autobiographical Writings*. Translated by Edmund Jephcott. New York: Schocken Books, 1986. NewYork: Schocken Books, 1978.
Bianquis, Geneviève. *Unzeitgemässe Betrachtungen – Considération Inactuelles*. Paris: Aubier, 1964.
Birringer, Johannes. *Theater, Theory, Postmodernism*. Bloomington: Indiana University Press, 1991.
Blanchot, Maurice. *The Book to Come*. Translated by Charlotte Mandell. Stanford: Stanford University Press, 2003.
———. *The Infinite Conversation*. Translated by Susan Hanson. Minneapolis: University of Minnesota Press. 1993.
———. *Le livre à venir*. Paris: Gallimard, 1959.
———. *L'entretien infini*. Paris: Gallimard 1969.
Blondel, Eric. *Nietzsche: le corps et la culture: la philosophie comme généalogie philologique* Paris: Presses Universitaires de France, 1986.
———. "Nietzsche: Life as Metaphor," in *The New Nietzsche*. Edited by David B. Allison. Cambridge: The MIT Press, 1997.
———. *Nietzsche: The Body and Culture: Philosophy as a Philological Genealogy*. Translated by Seán Hand. Stanford, California: Stanford University Press, 1991.
Boal, Augusto. *Teatro de Oprimido*. Rio de Janeiro: Civilização Brasileira, 1975.
———. *Theater of the Oppressed*. Translated by A. Charles and Maria-Odilia Leal McBride. New York: Theatre Communications Group, 1985. *Teatro de Oprimido*, 1974.
Borie, Monique. *Antonin Artaud: le théâtre et le retour aux sources*. Paris: Gallimard, 1989.
Brecht, Bertold. "On the Use of Music in an Epic Theatre," in *Gesammelte Werke*, 15, 476; in *Brecht on Theatre: The Development of an Aesthetic*. Translated by John Willet. New York: Hill and Wang, 1964.
Bröckers, Mathias and Paul Schreyer. *Wir Sind die Guten*. Frankfurt/Main: Westend Verlag, 2014.
Brzoza, Halina. *Достоевский. Просторы Движущегося Сознания*. Poznań: Wydawnictwo Naukowe Uniwersytetu im Adama Mickiewicza, 1992.
———. *Dostojewski. Między mitem, tragedią i apokalipsą*. Poznań: Wydawnictwo Uniwersytetu Mikołaja Kopernika, 1995.

Buckle, Henry Thomas. *History of Civilization in England*. New York: D. Appleton and Company, 1875.
Bulgakov, S. N. "Русскайа Трагедиа," in *Бесы: Антология русской критики*. Edited by L. Saraskina. Москва: Согласие, 1996.
Burckhardt, Jacob. *The Greeks and the Greek Civilisation*. Translated by Sheila Stern. New York: St. Marti's Press, 1998.
Camus, Albert. *Le myth de Sisyphe. Essai sur l'absurde*. Paris: Gallimard, 1942.
———. *The Myth of Sisyphus and Other Essays*. Translated by Justin O'Brien. New York: Vintage International, 1991.
Caron, Michel and Serge Rutin. *Les Alchimistes*. Paris: Éditions du Seuil, 1959.
Carr, Karen L. *The Banalization of Nihilism: Twentieth-Century Responses to Meaninglessness*. Albany: State University of New York Press, 1992.
Chernyshevsky, Nikolay Gavrilovich. *What Is to Be Done: Tales of the New People*. Translated by Laura Beraha. Moscow: Raduga, 1983.
———. *Что делать?* Москба: Дрофа, 2009.
Chestov Léon. (See Shestov).
Cicovacki, Predrag. 2012. *Dostoevsky and the Affirmation of Life*. New Brunswick: Transaction Publishers.
Clemens, Justin and Chris Feik. "Nihilism, Tonight...," in *Nihilism Now: Monsters of Energy*. Edited by K. Ansel-Pearson and D. Morgan. New York: St. Martin's Press Inc., 2000.
Clifford, James. "On Collecting Art and Culture," in *The Cultural Studies Reader*. Edited by Simon During. London, New York: Rutledge, 1993.
Coetzee, J. M. *The Master of Petersburg*. New York: Penguin Books, 1994.
Courtine, Jean-François. Entry "Res," in *Dictionary of Untranslatables: A Philosophical Lexicon*. Edited by Barbara Cassin, Translated by Emily Apter, Jacques Lezra, and Michael Wood. Princeton: Princeton University Press, 2014.
———. *Vocabulaire européen des philosophies: dictionaire des intraduisibles*. Paris: Seuil, 2004.
Cox, Roger L. "Kirillov, Stavrogin, and Suicide," in *Dostoevski and the Human Condition After a Century*. Edited by Alexej Urginsky, Frank S. Lambasa, and Valija K. Ozolins. New York, Westport, CT: Greenwood Press, 1986.
Curnier, Jean-Paul. *A Vif: Artaud, Nietzsche, Bataille, Pasolini, Sade, Klossowski*. Paris: Éditions Lignes & Manifestes, 2006.
Davison, Ray. *Camus: The Challenge of Dostoevsky*. Exeter: University of Exeter Press, 1997.
Del Caro, Adrian. "Symbolizing Philosophy: Ariadne and the Labyrinth," in *Nietzsche: Critical Assessments*. Edited by Daniel W. Conway. London, New York: Routledge, 1998.
Deleuze, Gilles. *Difference and Repetition*. Translated by Paul Patton. New York: Columbia University Press, 1994.
———. *Différence et repetition*. Paris: Presses Universitaires de France, 1968.
———. *Nietzsche*. Paris: Presses Universitaires de France, 1965.
———. *Nietzsche et la Philosophie*. Paris: Presses Universitaires de France, 1962.
———. *Nietzsche and Philosophy*. Translated by Hugh Tomlinson. New York: Columbia University Press, 1983.

———.*Qu'est.-ce que la philosophie*? Paris: Les Éditions de Minuit, 1991.———. "Nomad Thought," in *The New Nietzsche: Contemporary Styles of Interpretation*. Edited by Allison, David B. Cambridge, MA: The MIT Press (1985), 1997.

——— and Felix Guattari. *What Is Philosophy*? Translated by Hugh Tomlinson and Graham Burchell. New York: Columbia University Press, 1994.

de Man, Paul. *Allegories of Reading: Figural Language in Rousseau, Nietzsche, Rilke, and Proust*. New Haven and London: Yale University Press, 1979.

Denby, David. "Herder: Culture, Anthropology and the Enlightenment," *History of Human Sciences* (February 2005, 18).

Derrida, Jacques. *Dissemination*. Translated by Barbara Johnson. Chicago: The University of Chicago Press, 1981.

———. *Éperons: Les Styles de Nietzsche*. Paris: Flammarion, 1978.

———. *La dissémination*. Paris Éditions du Seuil, 1972.

———. *La vérité en peinture*. Paris: Flammarion, 1978.

———. *L'écriture et la différence*. Paris: Éditions du Seuil, 1967.

———. *Marges de la philosophie*. Paris: Les Éditions de Minuit, 1972.

———. *Margins of Philosophy*. Translated by Alan Bass. Chicago: The University of Chicago Press, 1982.

———. *Spurs: Nietzsche's Styles*. Translated by Barbara Harlow. Chicago: University of Chicago Press, 1979.

———. *The Truth in Painting*. Translated by Geoff Bennington and Ian McLeod. Chicago: The University of Chicago Press, 1987.

———. *Writing and Difference*. Translated by Alan Bass. Chicago: The University of Chicago Press, 1978.

Diels, Hermann and Walther Kranz. Editors. *Die Fragmente der Vorsokratiker*. Zürich: Weidmann, 1985.

Dostoevsky M. Fyodor. *The Brothers Karamazov*. Translated by Richard Pevear and Larrisa Volokhonsky. New York: Farrar, Straus and Giroux, 1990.

———. *Demons*. Translated by Richard Pevear and Larissa Volokhonsky. New York, Vintage Books, 1995.

———. *The Diary of a Writer*. Translated by Boris Brasol. New York: Charles Scribner's Sons, 1949.

———. *The House of the Dead*. Translated by David McDuff. London, New York: Penguin Classics 1985.

———. *The House of the Dead*. Translated by Constance Garnett. Mineola: Dover INC, 2004.

———. *Notes from a Dead House*. Translated by Richard Pevear and Larissa Volokhonsky. New York: Alfred A. Knopf, 2015.

———. *Notes from Underground*. Translated by Richard Pevear and Larrisa Volokhonsky. New York: Vintage Books, 1993.

———. *Записки из Мертвого Дома. Рассказы*. Москва: Советская Россия, 1983.

———. *Бесы, Роман в Трех Частях*. Москва: ТЕРРА, 2001.

———. *Записки из Подполья*. Москва: АСТ Астрель, 2006.

———. *Братья Карамазовы*. Москва: Эксмо, 2006.

———. "Записки из Мертвого Дома" in *Собрание Сочинений в девяти томах)*, vol. II, Москва: Астрель, 2006.

———. *Дниевник Писателя*. Москва: ЭКСМО, 2011.
Dryden, John. "Preface to *Ovid's Epistles*," in *The Works of John Dryden*. Edited by E. N. Hooker and H. T. Swedenberg Jr. vol. I Berkeley and Los Angeles: University of California Press, 1961.
Dumoulié, Camille. *Nietzsche et Artaud. Pour une éthique de la cruauté*. Paris: Presses Universitaires de France, 1992.
Eisnitz, Gail A. *Slaughterhouse: The Shocking Story of Greed, Neglect, an Inhumane TreatmentInside the U.S. Meat Industry*. New York: Prometheus Books, 2007.
Eliade, Mircea. Editor. *Forgerons et Alchimistes*. Paris: Champs-Flammarion, 1976.
Else, Gerald F. *Aristotle's Poetics: The Argument*. Cambridge, MA: Cambridge University Press, 1957.
———. *Plato and Aristotle on Poetry*. Edited by Peter Burian. Chapel Hill: The University of North Carolina Press. 1986.
Faye, Jean-Pierre and Michèle Cohen-Halimi. *L'histoire cachée du nihilisme: Jacobi, Dostoïevski, Heidegger, Nietzsche*. Paris: La Fabrique Éditions, 2008.
Fichte, Johann Gottlieb. *Introductions to the Wissenschaftslehre*. Translated and edited by Daniel Breazeale. Indianapolis: Hackett, 1994.
Fink, Eugen. *Nietzsches Philospphie*. Stuttgart: W. Kohlhammer GmbH. 1960.
———. *Nietzsche's Philosophy*. Translated by Goetz Richter. London, New York: Continuum, 2003.
———. *Spiel als Weltsymbol*. Stuttgart: W. Kohlhammer GmbH, 1960.
Ford, John. *'Tis Pity She's a Whore and Other Plays*. Edited by Marion Lomax. New York: Oxford University Press Inc., 1995.
Foucault, Michel. "Nietzsche, Freud, Marx," in *Cahiers de Royaumont: Nietzsche*. Paris: Les Éditions de Minuit, 1967.
———. "Nietzsche, Freud, Marx," in *Transforming the Hermeneutic Context: From Nietzsche to Nancy*. Edited by Gayle L. Ormiston. Albany: State University of New York Press, 1990.
———. "Nietzsche, Genealogy, History." Translated by Donald F. Bouchard and Sherry Simon, in *Foucault Reader*. Edited by Paul Rabinow. New York: Pantheon Books, 1984.
———. "Nietzsche, la généalogie, l'histoire," in *Dits et écrits I 1954–1975*. Paris: Gallimard, 1994.
———. "Theatrum Philosophicum," *Critique* 282 (November), 1970.
Franklyn, Julian. Editor. *A Survey of the Occult*. London: Arthur Barker, 1935.
Fraser, Giles. *Redeeming Nietzsche: On the Piety of Unbelief*. London, New York: Routledge, 2002.
Geertz, Clifford. *The Interpretation of Cultures: Selected Essays*. New York: Basic Books, 1973.
Gessen, S. I. "Трагедия зла (философский образ Ставрогина)," in *Бесы: Антология русской критики*. Edited by L. Saraskina. Москва: Согласие, 1996.
Gilbert-Lecomte, Roger. "La vie la mort le vide et le vent," in Antonin Artaud, *Œuvres Complètes*, vol. II, Paris: Gallimard, 1980.
Girard, René. *La Violence et le sacré*. Paris: Édition Bernard Grasset, 1972.

———. *Violence and the Sacre*. Translated by Patrick Gregory. Baltimore: The Johns Hopkins University Press, 1977.

Glucksmann, André. *Dostoïevski à Manhattan*. Paris: Robert Laffont, 2002.

———. *Ouest contre Ouest*. Paris: Plon, 2003.

Goethe, Johann Wolfgang von. *Goethe's Werke. Zwölfter Theil. Faust*. Wentworth Press, 2018.

Golsan, Richard J. "Preliminary Reflections on Anti-antiaméricanisme: André Glucksmann et compagnie," in *Contemporary French and Francophones Studies* 8:4, 2004.

Goodwin, James. *Confronting Dostoevsky's Demons: Anarchism and the Specter of Bakunin in Twentieth-Century Russia*. New York: Peter Lang Publishing Inc., 2011.

Green, Graham. *The Third Man*. London: Faber and Faber Ltd; Revised edition 1998.

Greene, Naomi. *Antonin Artaud: Poet without Words*. New York: Simon and Schuster, 1970.

Grotowski, Jerzy. "Il n'était pas entièrement lui-même," in *Les Temps Modernes* 251 (Avril) 1967.

Gus, Martin. *Understanding Terrorism*. Los Angeles: Sage Publications, Inc., 2015,

Haar, Michel. "Nietzsche and Metaphysical Language." Translated by Cyril and Liliane Welch. In *The New Nietzsche*. Edited by David B. Allison. Cambridge MA: The MIT Press, 1985.

Hamman, Johan Georg. *Writing on Philosophy and Language*. Cambridge: Cambridge University Press. 2007.

Hegel, G. W. F. *Phenomenology of Spirit*. Translated by A. V. Miller. Oxford: Oxford University Press, 1977.

Heidegger, Martin. *Hölderlins Hymne "Der Ister,"* Frankfurt am Main: Vittorio Klostermann GmbH, 1984.

———. *Hölderlin's Hymn "The Ister."* Translated by William McNeill and Julia Davis. Bloomington: Indiana University Press, 1996.

———. *Holzwege*. Frankfurt am Main: Vittorio Klostermann, 1950.

———. *Nietzsche I*. Translated by David Farrell Krell. San Francisco: Harper, 1991

———. *Nietzsche* II. Translated by David Farrell Krell. San Francisco: Harper, 1984.

———. *Nietzsche I and II*. Stuttgart: Günther Neske, 1961.

———. *Off the Beaten Track*. Edited and translated by Julian Young and Kenneth Haynes. Cambridge: Cambridge University Press, 2002.

———. *Poetry, Language, Thought*. Translated by Albert Hofstadter. New York: Harper & Row, 1975.

———. *Vorträge und Aufsätze*. Stuttgart: Günter Neske, 1954.

Herzen, Alexander. "Réponse à M. G. Wyrouboff," in *Supplément du Kolokol (La Cloche)*. Genève 15 Février, 1869.

Higgins, Kathleen M. *Nietzsche's Zarathustra*. Philadelphia: Temple University Press, 1987.

———. "Reading *Zarathustra*," in *Reading Nietzsche*. Edited by Solomon, Robert C. and Kathleen M. Higgins. N.Y., Oxford: Oxford University Press, 1988.

Hingley, Ronald. *The Undiscovered Dostoevsky*. London: Hamish Hamilton, 1962.

Hoghelande, de Theobald. *Liber de alchemiae dfficultatibus,* in *Theatrum Chemicum* Ursel: 1602.
Hölderlin, Friedrich. *Poems and Fragments.* Translated by Michael Hamburger. Ann Arbor: University of Michigan Press, 1967.
Homer. *Odyssey.* Greek text with English translation by A. T. Murray (1919) revised by George. E. Dimock. Cambridge MA: Harvard University Press, 1998.
Horkheimer, Max and Theodor W. Adorno. *Dialectic of Enlightenment.* Edited by Gunzelin Schmid Noerr. Translated by Edmund Jephcott. New York: Seabury Press, 1972.
———. *Gesammelte Schriften,* Band 3: *Dialektik der Aufklärung: Philosophische Fragmente,* Frankfurt am Main: Suhrkamp, 1981.
Ivanov, Vyacheslav. "Достоевский и роман-трагедия," *Русская мысль,* 1911, Кн. 5, reprinted in: *О Достоевском: Творчество Достоевского в русской мысли 1881–1931 годов,* Москва: КНИГА, 1990.
———. *Freedom and the Tragic Life: A Study in Dostoevsky.* Translated by Norman Cameron. New York: The Noonday Press, 1957.
Jackson, Robert Louis. *The Art of Dostoevsky, Deliriums and Nocturnes.* Princeton NJ: Princeton University Press, 1981.
———. *Dialogues with Dostoevsky. The Overwhelming Questions.* Stanford: Stanford University Press, 1993.
———. *Dostoevsky's Quest for Form: A Study in His Philosophy of Art.* New Haven: Yale University Press, 1966.
———. *Dostoevsky's Underground Man in Russian Literature.* The Hague: Mouton & Co., 1958.
Jacobi, Friedrich, Heinrich. *Allwill.* Groningen, Djakarta: J. B. Wolters, 1957.
———. *Die Schriften.* Edited by Leo Matthias. Berlin: Verlag die Schmiede, 1926.
———. *Fliegende Blätter und andere Sentenzen.* Heidelberg: Sauer-Verlag. 1965.
———. *The Main Philosophical Writings and the Novel* Allwill. Translated by George di Giovanni. Montreal & Kingston: McGill-Queen's University Press, 1994.
———. *Werke, Dritter Band.* Leipzig: Gerhard Fleischer, 1816.
Janicaud, Dominique. "La postérité des *Possédés*: quel nihilism?" in *Nietzsche et le temps des nihilismes.* Edited by Jean-François Mattéi. Paris: Presses Universitaires de France, 2005.
Johst, Hanns. *Schlageter.* Stuttgard: Akademischer Verlar H.-D. Heinz, 1984.
Jung, Carl Gustav. *The Collected Works.* Translated by R.F.C. Hull. London: Routledge, 1953.
———. *Gesammelte Werke.* Oiten: Walter-Verlag, Vol. 12, 1972.
Kant, Immanuel. *Critique of Pure Reason.* Translated by Norman Kemp Smith. New York: St. Martin's Press, 1965.
———. "Kritik der reinen Vernunft," vol. I–IV in *Herausgegeben von Wilhelm Weischedel* in XII vol. Frankfurt am Main: Suhrkamp, 1974.
Kaufmann, Walter. *Nietzsche: Philosopher, Psychologist, Antichrist.* Princeton: Princeton University Press (1950), 1974.
———. *Tragedy and Philosophy.* Princeton: Princeton University Press (1968), 1992.

Kirk, Irina. *Dostoevskij and Camus. The Themes of Consciousness, Isolation, Freedom and Love*. München: Wilhelm Fink Verlag, 1974.

Kluckhohn, Clyde. *Mirror for Man: The Relation of Anthropology to Modern Life*. New York: Whittlesey House, 1949.

Knapp, Bettina L. *Theater and Alchemy*. Detroit: Wayne State University Press. 1980.

Knapp, Liza. *The Annihilation of Inertia. Dostoevsky and Metaphysics*. Evanstone, IL: Northwestern University Press, 1996.

Lacan, Jacques. *Le séminaire, livre VII: L'éthique de la psychanalyse*. Paris: Éditions du Seuil, 1986.

Lacoue-Labarthe, Philippe. *La poésie comme experience*. Paris: Christian Bourgois Éditeur, 1986.

———. *Le sujet de la Philosophie. Typographies I*. Paris: Aubier-Flammarion, 1979.

———. *Poetry as Experience*. Translated by Andrea Tarnowski. Stanford CA: Stanford University Press, 1999.

———. *The Subject of Philosophy*. Edited by T. Trezise. Minneapolis: University of Minnesota Press, 1993.

Lampert, Laurence. *Nietzsche's Teaching: An Interpretation of Thus Spoke Zarathustra*. New Haven: Yale University Press, 1986.

Land, Nick. "Aborting the Human Race," in *The Fate of the New Nietzsche*. Edited by Keith Ansell-Pearson and Howard Caygill. Aldershot, England: Averbury, 1993.

Lawrence, D. H. "The Novel and the Feelings," in *Phoenix: The Posthumous Papers of D. H. Lawrence*. Edited by Edward D. McDonald. New York: Penguin Books, 1980.

Leiter, Brian. *Nietzsche on Morality*. London: Routledge, 2002.

Lemm, Vanessa. *Nietzsche's Animal Philosophy: Culture, Politics, and the Animality of the Human Being*. New York: Fordham University Press, 2009.

Lessing, G. E. *Hamburg Dramaturgy*. Translated by Helen Zimmern. 1890, reprint New York: Dover Publications, 1962.

———. *Hamburgische Dramaturgie: Kritisch Durchgesehene Gesamtausgabe mit Einleitung und Kommentar von Otto Mann*. Stuttgart: Alfred Kroner Verlag, 1963.

Lewis, Jeff. *Cultural Studies: the Basics*. London: SAGE Publications Ltd., 2008.

Löwith, Karl. *Von Hegel zu Nietzsche. Der revolutionäre Bruch im Denken des neunzehnten Jahrhunderts*. Hamburg: Felix Meiner Verlag, 1995.

Mallarmé, Stéphane. *Œuvres complètes*. Paris: Gallimard, 1945.

———. *Collected Poems*. Translated by Henry Weinfields. Berkeley: University of California Press, bilingual edition, 1994.

———. *Selected Poetry and Prose*. Edited by Mary Ann Caws. New York: A New Directions Book, 1982.

Mandalios, John. *Nietzsche and the Necessity of Freedom*. Lanham: Lexington Books, 2008.

Marx, Karl. "Theses on Feuerbach," in *Selected Writings*. Edited by Lawrence H. Simon. Indianapolis: Hackett Publishing Company, 1994.

Mattéi, Jean-François. *L'Étranger et le simulacre: essai sur la fondation de l'ontologie platonicienne*. Paris: Presses Universitaires de France, 1983.

———. Editor. *Nietzsche et le temps de nihilismes*. Paris: Presses Universitaires de France, 2005.

Mencken, H. L. *The Philosophy of Friedrich Nietzsche*. Tucson AR: Sharp Press, 2003.
Mikhailovsky, Nikolai K. *Dostoevsky: A Cruel Talent*. Translated by Spencer Cadmus. Ann Arbor: Ardis, 1978.
Mochulsky, Konstantin. *Достоевский: жизнь и творчество*. Париж: YMCA Press, 1947.
———. *Dostoevsky: His Life and Work*. Translated by Michael A. Minihan. Princeton NJ: Princeton University Press, 1967.
Müller-Lauter, Wolfgang." The Spirit of Revenge and the Eternal Recurrence: On Heidegger's Later Interpretation of Nietzsche," in *Nietzsche Critical Assessments*. Edited by Daniel W. Conway. London, New York: Routledge, 1998.
Myftiu, Bessa. *Nietzsche & Dostoïevski éducateurs*. Nice: Éditions Paradigme, 2004.
Natov, Nadine. "Albert Camus' Attitude toward Dostoevsky." *Revue de Littérature Compareé*, No 3–4, 1981.
Nechaev, Sergey. *Catechism of a Revolutionist*. www.uoregon.edu/~kimball/Nqv.
Nehamas, Alexander. *Nietzsche: Life and Literature*. Cambridge: Harvard University Press, 1985.
Nemcová Banerjee, Maris. *Dostoevsky: The Scandal of Reason*. Great Barrington, MA: Lindisfarne Books, 2006.
Neyrat, Frédéric. *Le terrorisme, un concept piégé*. Alfortville: Éditions éRe, 2011.
Nietzsche, Friedrich. *The Anti-Christ, Ecce Homo, Twilight of the Idols and Other Writings*. Edited by Aaron Ridley and Judith Norman. Translated by Judith Norman. Cambridge: Cambridge University Press, 2005.
———. *Basic Writings of Nietzsche*. Translated and edited by Walter Kaufmann. New York: The Modern Library, 1966.
———. *Beyond Good and Evil*. Edited by Rolf-Peter Horsman and Judith Norman. Translated by Judith Norman. Cambridge: Cambridge University Press, 2005.
———. *The Birth of Tragedy and Other Writings*. Edited by Raymond Geuss and Ronald Speirs. Translated by Ronald Speirs. Cambridge: Cambridge University Press, 1999.
———. *Briefe: Januar 1880–Dezember 1884*. Edited by Giorgio Colli and Mazzino Montinari. Berlin, New York: Walter de Gruyter. 1981.
———. *Briefe: Januar 1887–Januar 1889*. Edited by Giorgio Colli and Mazzino Montinari. Berlin, New York: Walter de Gruyter1984.
———. *Briefe: September 1864–April 1869*. Berlin: Walter de Gruyter, 1975.
———. *Briefwechsel, Kritische Gesamtausgabe*. Berlin: Walter de Gruyter, 1981.
———. *Day Break: Thoughts on the Prejudices of Morality*. Edited by Maudemarie Clark and Brian Leiter. Translated by R. J. Hollingdale. Cambridge: Cambridge University Press, 1997.
———. *Der Wille zur Macht*. Stuttgart: Alfred Kröner Verlag, 1996.
———. *The Gay Science*. Translated by Josephine Nauckhoff. Cambridge: Cambridge University Press, 2001.
———. *Gesammelte Werke*. Edited by Max Oehler. München: Musarion Verlag, 1920.
———. *Human All to Human*. Translated by R. J. Hollngdale. Cambridge: Cambridge University Press, 1996.

———. *Kritische Studienausgabe*, in 15 Bänden. Edited by Giorgio Colli und Mazzino Montinari. Berlin, New York: de Gruyter, 1967–77.
———. *On the Genealogy of Morality*. Edited by Keith Ansell-Pearson. Translated by Carol Diethe. Cambridge: Cambridge University Press, 2006.
———. *On the Genealogy of Morals and Ecce Homo*. Translated by Walter Kaufmann and R. J. Hollingdale. New York: Vintage Books, 1989.
———. *Philosophy in the Tragic Age of the Greeks*. Translated by Marianne Cowan. Washington, DC: Regnery Publishing, Inc., 1962.
———. *The Portable Nietzsche*. Translated and edited by Walter Kaufmann. New York: Viking Penguin, 1954.
———. *Thus Spake Zarathustra*. Translated by Thomas Common, revised by H. James Birx. New York: Prometheus Books, 1993.
———. *Thus Spoke Zarathustra*. Translated by Adrian del Caro. Cambridge: Cambridge University Press, 2006.
———. *Twilight of the Idols*. Translated by Duncan Large. Oxford, New York: Oxford University Press, 1998.
———. *Untimely Meditations*. Translated by R. J. Hollingdale. Edited by Daniel Breazeale. Cambridge: Cambridge University Press, 1997.
———. *The Will to Power*. Translated by Walter Kaufmann and R. J. Hollingdale. New York: Vintage Books, 1968.
———. *Writings from Late Notebooks*. Edited by Rüdiger Bittner. Translated by Kate Struge. Cambridge: Cambridge University Press. 2003.
Nishimura, Kuniyuki. "E. H. Carr Dostoevsky, and the Problem of Irrationality in Modern Europe." *International Relations* 25:1, 2011.
Oksenberg Rorty, Amelie. Editor. *Aristotle's Poetics*. Princeton: Princeton University Press, 1992.
Owen, David, and Aaron Ridley. "Dramatis Personae: Nietzsche, Culture, and Human Types," in *Why Nietzsche Still?* Edited by Alan D. Schrift. Berkeley: University of California Press, 2000
Paperno, Irina. *Suicide as a Cultural institution in Dostoevsky's Russia*. Ithaca: Cornell University Press. Paperno, Irina. 1997.
Patterson, Charles. *Eternal Treblinka: Our Treatment of Animals and the Holocaust*. New York: Lantern Books, 2002.
Perloff, Marjorie. *The Poetics of Indeterminacy: Rimbaud to Cage*. Evanston, IL: Northwestern University Press, 1999.
Plato. *The Collected Dialogues of Plato*. Edited by Edith Hamilton and Huntington Cairns. Princeton: Princeton University Press 1961.
———. *Complete Works*. Edited by John M. Cooper. Indianapolis: Hackett Publishing Company, 1997.
———. *The Dialogues of Plato*. Translated by Jowett. Reprint, New York: Random House (1892), 1937.
———. *Gorgias*. Translated by Terence Irwin. New York: Oxford University Press, 1979.
———. *Oeuvres Complètes*. Translated by Léon Robin. Paris: Gallimard, 1950.
———. *Opera*. Edited by Johannes Burnet. Reprint, Oxford: Oxford University Press (1902), 1989.

———. *Phèdre*. Translated by Luc Brisson. Paris: Flammarion, 1989.

———. *The Republic*. Edited by G. R. F. Ferrari. Translated by Tom Griffith. Cambridge: Cambridge University Press 2000.

———. *The Republic of Plato*. Translated by Francis M. Cornford. Reprint, London: Oxford University Press (1941) 1973.

———. *The Republic of Plato*. Translated by Alan Bloom. Reprint. New York: Basic Books (1968) 1991.

———. *Theaetetus. Sophist*. Greek text with an English translation by Harold North Fowler. Reprint, Cambridge, MA: Harvard University Press (1921), 1996.

———. *Two Comic Dialogues: Ion and Hippias Major*. Translated by Paul Woodruff. Indianapolis: Hackett Publishing Company, 1983.

Ponton, Olivier. "Le 'caractère équivoque' du nihilism: l'analyse nietzschéenne de la croyance et du scepticisme dans le fragments de 1887–1888," in *Nietzsche et le temps de nihilismes*. Edited by Jean-François Mattéi. Paris: Presses Universitaires de France, 2005.

Puchner, Martin. "The Theater in Modernist Thought," *New Literary History*, 33:3 (Summer 2002).

Rimbaud, Arthur. *Poésies, Une saison en enfer. Illuminations*. Paris: Gallimard, 1984.

Roberts, Tyler T. *Contesting Spirit: Nietzsche, Affirmation, Religion*. Princeton: Princeton University Press, 1998.

Rosen, Stanley. *Limits of Analysis*. New York: Basic Books, 1980.

———. *Nihilism: A Philosophical Essay*. New Haven: Yale University Press, 1982.

Rosset, Clément. *Joyful Cruelty: Toward a Philosophy of the Real*. Edited and translated by David F. Bell. New York, Oxford: Oxford University Press. 1993.

———. *Le Principe de cruauté*. Paris: Minuit, 1988.

Rotrou, Jean de. *Le Véritable Saint Genest*. Edited by François Bonfils and Emmanuelle Hénin. Paris: Flammarion, 1999.

Saraskina, Liudmila. *Бесы: Роман предупреждение*. Москва: Советский Писатель, 1990.

———. Editor. *Бесы: Антологиа русской критики*. Москва: Согласие, 1996.

Sartarelli, Stephen. "Where Did Our Love Go," *The Nation* (January 12/19, 2004).

Scanlan, James P. *Dostoevsky the Thinker*. Ithaca: Cornell University Press, 2002.

Schutte, Ofelia. *Beyond Nihilism: Nietzsche without Masks*. Chicago: The University of Chicago Press, 1984.

Sellin, Eric. *The Dramatic Concepts of Antonin Artaud*. Chicago: The University of Chicago Press, 1968.

Seneca, Lucius Annaeus. *Epistulae Morales*. Vol. II. With English translation by Richard M. Gummere. Cambridge, MA: Harvard University Press.

Shakespeare, William. "A Midsummer Night's Dream," in *The Riverside Shakespeare*. Boston: Houghton Mifflin Company, 1974.

———. "The History of Troilus and Cressida," in *The Riverside Shakespeare*. Boston: Houghton Mifflin Company, 1974.

Shestov (Chestov Leon), Lev. *Dostoevsky, Tolstoy and Nietzsche*. Edited by Bernard Martin. Athens: Ohio University Press, 1969.

———. *La philosophie de la tragedie: Dostoïevski et Nietzsche*. Paris: Le Bruit du Temps, 2012.

———. *Speculation and Revelation*. Translated by Bernard Martin. Athens: Ohio University Press, 1982.
———. *Умозрение и откровение*. Paris: YMCA Press, 1964.
———. *Достоевский и Ницше (философия трагедии)*. Москва, АСТ, 2007.
———. and Jean-Luc Nancy. In *Europe, revue littéraire mensuel*. No 960/Avril, 2009.
Smyth, Herbert, Weir. *Greek Grammar*. Cambridge: Harvard University Press, 1956.
Soll, Ivan. "Pessimism and the Tragic View of Life: Reconsiderations of Nietzsche's *Birth of Tragedy*," in *Reading Nietzsche*. Edited by Solomon, Robert C. and Kathleen M. Higgins. NewYork, Oxford: Oxford University Press, 1988.
Solomon, Robert C. Editor. *Nietzsche: A Collection of Critical Essays*. Edited by Robert. Notre Dame: University of Notre Dame Press, 1980.
———. and Kathleen M. Higgins. Editors. *Reading Nietzsche*. New York, Oxford: Oxford University Press, 1988.
Sophocles. *Antigone*. Edited and translated by Hugh Lloyd-Jones. Cambridge MA: Harvard University Press. 1994, vol. II.
———. "Antigone". In *Greek Tragedies*. Vol. 1. Edited by David Green and Richmond Lattimore. Chicago: The University of Chicago Press, 1991.
Spiegel, Marjorie. *The Dreaded Comparison: Human and Animal Slavery*. New York: Mirror Books., 1996.
Stern, Sheila. *The Greeks and Greek Civilization*. New York: St. Marti's Press, 1998.
Swift, Jonathan. "The Battel of the Books," in *The Writings of Jonathan Swift*. Edited by Robert A. Grennberg and Wlliam B. Piper. New York, London: W. W. Norton & Company, 1973.
Tabucchi, Antonio. "Éloge de la Littérature." *Italies*, No Special, 2007.
Tonelli, Franco. *L'Esthétique de la cruauté*. Paris: A.-G. Nizet, 1972
Turgenev, Ivan. *Fathers and Sons* Translated by Ralph E. Mattlaw. New York, London: W. W. Norton & Company, 1966.
———. *Отцы и Дети*. Москба: АСТ, 2009.
———. *Väter und Söhne*. Berlin: Insel-Verlag, 1958.
Turner, Victor. *From Ritual to Theater: The Human Seriousness of Play*. New York: PAJ Publications, 1982.
Tylor, E. B. *Primitive Culture: Researches into the Development of Mythology, Philosophy, Religion, Language, Art and Custom*. London: John Murray, New York: G.P. Putnam's Sons, 1920.
Valentino, Russell S. "The Word Made Flesh in Dostoevskii's *Possessed*" in *Slavic Review*, 56:1 (Spring, 1997).
Valéry, Paul. *Œuvres*. Paris: Gallimard, Bibliotheque de la Pleiade, 1957.
———. *Variété II*. Paris: Gallimard, 1930.
Vattimo, Gianni. *The End of Modernity. Nihilism and Hermeneutics in Postmodern Culture*. Translated by Jon R. Snyder. Baltimore: The Johns Hopkins University Press, 1988.
———. *La fine della modernità. Nichilismo ed ermeneutica nella cultura post-moderna: un significativo contributo all'attuale dibattito filosofico*. Milano: Garzanti, 1985.
Varro, *On the Latin Language*. Latin text with English translation by Roland G. Kent. Cambridge, MA: Harvard University Press, VI, 1958.

Virgil. *Aeneid.* Translated by Robert Fitzgerald. New York: Vintage Classics a division of Random House, 1990.
Vonnegut, Kurt. *Slaughterhouse 5.* New York: Dial Press Trade, 2009.
Weisse, Christian Felix. *Richard der Dritte, Ein Trauerspiel in Fünf Aufzügen.* Wentworth Press, 2018.
Woolfolk, Alan. "The Two Switchmen of Nihilism: Dostoevsky and Nietzsche," *Mosaic* 22:1 (Winter, 1989).
Yeats, W. B. *Selected Criticism.* Edited by A. Norman Jeffares (1964) London: Pan Books-Macmillan, 1976.
Zabriskie-Temple, Ruth. *The Critic's Alchemy. A Study of the Introduction of French Symbolism into England.* New Haven, CT: College and University Press, 1953.

Works to Consult

Agamben, Giorgio. *Il linguaggio e la morte: Un seminario sul luogo della negatività*, Torino: Giulio Einaudi editore. 1982.
———. *Language and Death: The Place of Negativity*. Translated by Karen E. Pinkus and Michael Hardt. Minneapolis: University of Minnesota Press, 1991.
———. *Homo Sacer: Il potere sovrano e la nuda vita*, Torino: Giulio Einaudi editore, 1995.
———. *Homo Sacer: Sovereign Power and Bare Life*. Translated by Daniel Heller-Roazen. Stanford: Stanford University Press, 1998.
———.*Quel che resta di Auschwitz: L'archivio e il testimone*. Torino:Bollati Boringhieri, 1998.
———. *Remnants of Auschwitz: The Witness and the Archive*. Translated by Daniel Heller-Roazen. New York: Zone Books, 1999.
Arendt, Hannah. *On Violence*. Orlando, New York: Harvest Book Harcourt Inc., 2014.
Baron-Cohen, Simon. *The Science of Evil: On Empathy and the Origins of Cruelty*. Philadelphia PA, 2011
Benjamin, Walter. "Zur Kritik der Gewalt," in *Schriften*, Band I, Frankfurt am Main: Suhrkamp Verlag, 1955.
———. *The Origin of German Tragic Drama*. Translated by John Osborne. London: Verso, 1977.
———. "Critique of Violence," in *Reflections: Essays, Aphorisms, Autobiographical Writings*. Translated by Edmund Jephcott. New York: Schocken Books, 1986.
Bernasconi, Robert. "Literary Attestation in Philosophy: Heidegger's Footnote on Tolstoy's 'The Death of Ivan Ilyich,'" in *Heidegger in Question: The Art of Existing*. Atlantic Highlands, NJ: Humanities Press, 1993.
Calarco, Matthew. *Zoographies: The Question of the Animal from Heidegger to Derrida*. New York: Columbia University Press, 2008.
Castro, Marina de. *Terreur, un concept psycho-stratégique*. Paris : Éditions l'Hermattan, 2017.

Conway, Daniel W. "Heidegger, Nietzsche, and the Origins of Nihilism." *Journal of Nietzsche Studies* 3 (Spring), 1992.

———. and Peter S. Groff. Eds. *Nietzsche: Critical Assessments*. London, New York: Routledge, 1998.

Debord Guy. *La Société du Spectacle*, Paris: Gallimard 1992.

———. *The Society of the Spectacle*. Translated by Donald Nicholson-Smith. New York: Zone Books, 1995.

Dostoevsky M. Fyodor. "The Gambler," in *Great Short Works of Fyodor Dostoevsky*. Edited by Ronald Hingley. New York: Perennial Classics, 1968.

———. *(Игрок* in *Собрание Сочинений в десяти томах,* vol. IV. Москва: Государственное Издательстбо Художестбенной Литературы.

Foucault, Michel. *Surveiller et punir. Naissance de la prison*, Paris: Gallimard, 1975.

———. *Discipline & Punish. The Birth of the Prison*. Translated by Alan Sheridan. NewYork: Vintage Books, 1995.

Girard, René. *Resurrection from the Underground. Feodor Dostoevsky*. Edited and translated by James G. Williams. East Lansing: Michigan State University Press, 2012.

Kuhn, Elisabeth. *Friedrich Nietzsches Philosophie des europäischen Nihilismus*. Berlin: Walter de Gruyter, 1992.

Levin, Iu. D. *Шекспир и русская литература XIX века*. Leningrad: Nauka, 1988.

Motaigne, Michel de. "On Cruelty," in *The Essays of Michel de Montaigne*. Translated and Edited by M. A. Screech. New York: Allen Lane, the Penguin Press, 1991.

Nelson, Maggie. *The Art of Cruelty*. New York: W. W. Norton & Company, 2012.

Plato. *Laws*. Translated by R. G. Bury. Reprint, Cambridge, MA: Harvard University Press, (1926) 1984.

———. *Timaeus, Critias*. Translated by R. G. Bury. Reprint, Cambridge, MA: Harvard University Press, (1929) 1989.

———. *Laches, Protagoras, Meno, Euthydemus*. Greek text with an English translation by W. R. M. Lamb. Cambridge, MA: Harvard University Press, 1937.

———. *Plato's Phaedrus*. Translated by R. Hackforth. Cambridge: Cambridge University Press, 1952.

———. *Symposium*. Translated by Alexander Nehamas and Paul Woodruff. Indianapolis: Hackett Publishing Company, 1989.

———. *Phaedrus*. Translated by Alexander Nehamas and Paul Woodruff. Indianapolis: Hackett Publishing Company, 1995.

Taylor, Kathleen. *Cruelty, Human Evil and the Human Brain*. Oxford, NY: Oxford University Press, 2009.

Thévenin, Paule. *Antonin Artaud, ce Désespéré qui vous parle*. Paris: Seuil, 1993.

Tine, Val N. *Nothing or Everything*. Copyright by Val N. Tine, 2017.

Villiers de L'Isle-Adam. *Contes Cruels*. Paris: Bordas, 1989.

Wiesel, Elie. *La nuit*. Paris: Les Éditions De Minuit, 1958.

———. *Night*. Translated by Marion Wiesel. New York: Hill and Wang, 2006.

Wolting, Patrick. *Nietzsche et le problème de la civilisation*. Paris: Presses Universitaires de France, 1995.

Žižek, Slavoj. *Violence: Six Sideways Reflections*. New York: Picador, 2008.

Index

abstractedness, 42, 51–52
abyss, 65
Adelman, Gary, 56n44, 56n60
Aeschylus, 48, 66
aesthetics, 68–69, 73, 78, 82, 85n54
Agamben, Giorgio, 82, 89n139, 89n154
Albrecht, Thomas, 36n92
alchemy, 74–76, 78, 80, 87n95, 87n98, 88n136, 89n143
Alejandro, Roberto, 37n110
alêtheia. See truth
Alleau, René. 75, 87n105
Allison, David B., 38n124
Althusser, Louis, 61, 84n15
ambiguity, 31, 40–41, 47, 53, 91–92
anarchy, 7, 65–66, 70, 72, 76–77, 83, 85n49
animal, 6–7, 18–21, 26, 30, 34n38, 93
annihilation, 7, 14, 48
Antigone, 6–7, 10n40, 66
apocalyptic*apokalupsis*, 70
Apollo, 15, 25, 27–28, 32n14, 36n92
appearance, 22, 26, 35n80, 38n123, 50, 66, 77
Aristotle, 6, 41–42, 44, 55n27, 59–62, 67, 69–72, 81, 84n16, 86n91
arkhê. See principle
Arnold, Matthew, 2–5, 9n16, 10n25, 11–15, 20, 65

art, 1, 6–7, 15–17, 19, 21, 24–25, 28, 36n92, 36n94, 39–42, 44, 46, 52, 53n5, 54n20, 55n39, 60–61, 66–67, 69, 71–73, 75, 77, 80, 83, 83n6, 88n136, 92–93
Artaud, Antonin, 1, 6–8, 9n3, 10n41, 59–71, 73, 76–92
Aufhebung. See overcoming, *relève*
Auschwitz, 92

Babich, Babette E. 7, 19, 34n37, 34n38, 38n120
Bacon, Roger, 75, 87n107
Bakunin, Mikhail, 44
barrier. *See* limitation
Baudelaire, Charles, 73, 87n97
Baudrillard, Jean, 5, 10n33
beauty, 25, 49–50
being, 4, 6–7, 10n30, 12, 16, 19, 21–25, 28, 30, 41–43, 52, 54n24, 60–62, 71–72, 75, 86n81
belief, 1, 3, 38n123, 40, 51–53, 58n110, 65
Benjamin, Walter, 10n27
Bildung. See culture, education, formation
Blanchot, Maurice, 35n80, 38n122, 60, 84n10
Blondel, Eric, 11, 32n2, 35n74, 37n110

blood, 3, 7, 10n41, 18, 20, 22, 31, 39, 49, 53n6, 59–60, 65, 71, 74, 77, 91, 93
Boal, Augusto, 66, 84n16, 85n47
body, 9n7, 18, 40, 53n5, 63, 69, 72–75, 77, 79
borders. *See* limitatons
boredom, 76, 92
boundary, *See* limitation
Brecht, Bertold, 61, 63, 81
brutality, 61
Brzoza, Halina, 58n112
Buckle, Henry T., 2–3, 22
Bulgakov, S. N., 49, 57n78
Burke, Edmund, 77

camel, 30–31
Camus, Albert, 8, 39, 41–43, 48, 51, 54n19, 54n20, 55n28, 55n38, 57n71, 57n93, 58n110, 63, 92
Caron, Michel, 75, 87n101
Carr, Karen L., 41, 55n29
Cassirer, Ernst, 2
catharsis. *See* purification
chaos, 63, 66, 69–71, 74, 76–78, 83, 85n44
character, 7, 16, 24–27, 32, 37n103, 39, 41, 43–44, 46–50, 56n60, 61, 63, 66–70, 74, 77–82
chemistry, 74, 76, 87n95
Chernyshevsky, Nikolay G., 4
Chestov, Leon. *See* Shestov
Cicovacki, Predrag, 48, 57n74
city, 40, 63, 66–67, 72
civilization, 1–2, 8n2, 29, 54n25, 59, 76
closure, 64, 86n80
Coetzee, J. M., 44, 56n44
communication, 68
concealment, 78
concept, 2–4, 7, 14, 41–42, 44, 55n29, 56n43, 62, 72–73, 82, 85n54, 86n91, 91
coniunctio, 74, 79
conscience, 18–21, 24, 78
consciousness, 10n40, 21, 40, 64, 75, 78

contemplation, 67–68, 71, 81
contradiction, 31, 38n122, 47, 60, 77, 83n9
conundrum, 47, 60
corruption, 22–23
cosmodicy, 67
cosmology, 66, 74
cosmos. *See* world, universe, order
Cox, Roger L., 56n62
creation, 7, 21, 25–27, 30, 34n51, 45, 62, 64, 71, 86n74
crime, 10n40, 61, 63, 65, 73
cruelty, vii, 5–8, 10–11, 13–40, 48–49, 52, 59–71, 73, 76–83, 86n74, 89n140, 91–93
cruor. *See* blood
culture, 1–8, 8n1–5, 9n16, 9n20, 10n30, 10n34, 11–21, 25, 28–32, 32n3, 33n15, 39, 40, 42, 50, 59–60, 65–66, 83, 83n2, 83n6, 91–93
Curnier, Jean-Paul, 5, 10n34, 80, 89n140

dancing, 29
danger, 7, 21, 23, 36n92, 40–42, 45, 52, 60–62, 64–67, 69–71, 77–80, 92
Darwin, Charles, 12
Davison, Ray, 48, 57n72
death, 19, 21, 28–29, 46–48, 50, 52–53, 63, 65, 72, 89n155, 93
decadent, 15, 76
degeneration, 6, 83
Deleuze, Gilles, 5–6, 8n1, 10n35, 30, 35n72, 37n103, 37n112, 54n19, 56n43, 88n125, 85n130
Derrida, Jacques, 37n116, 59, 83n1, 83n3, 86n80
Descartes, René, 73
desire, 4, 8, 9n15, 10n30, 16, 21, 27, 50, 59, 92
destiny, 7, 29, 53, 63, 75
destruction, 16, 21, 47–49
Deutschland, 93
difference, 6, 8, 10n35, 14, 47, 52–53, 60, 65, 71, 73, 87n91, 88n130, 92–93

Dionysus, 15, 32n14
disgust, 61
disintegration, 63
disorder, 63–64, 66, 70, 76–77
dissonance, 70, 77, 88n120
Dostoevsky Fyodor M.: *Demons*, 4, 42–44, 46–48, 50, 52, 55n31, 56n46; *Notes from Underground*, 40, 45, 52, 56n54; *The House of the Dead*, 45–46
Doxa. *See* opinion
dragon, 17, 30–31, 74
drama, 17, 76–77
Dumoulié, Camille, 7, 10n41

education, 11, 67
eidos. *See* idea
eikôn. *See* image, representation
Eisnitz, Gail A., 7, 19
eleos. *See* pity
elevation, 64
Eliade, Mircea, 74, 87n96
Eliot, Gerald F., 73
Enlightenment, 1–2, 4, 6–7, 12, 14, 18, 22, 61
epistemological, 45, 70, 73
ergon, 3–4, 37n116, 48
error, 4, 17, 24, 67
essence, 10n42, 40, 76, 87n108
ethics, 16
Euripides, 15
evil, vii, 6, 11, 13–14, 17, 19, 23–25, 28, 30, 36n95, 43, 45, 49, 67, 76, 92.
existence, 16–18, 27, 32, 34n51, 40, 59, 64, 71, 80, 83n2, 89n140
exorcism, 64, 68
experience, 8, 12–13, 16, 25, 31, 37n103, 37n109, 39, 42–46, 49, 53n6, 55n26, 63–65, 69–72, 77–80, 92

fate, 48, 64
fault, 3, 67
fear, 19, 21, 25, 28, 48, 52, 61–62, 65, 82

Fichte, Johann G., 41, 54n15
fire, 63, 74, 76–78
Ford, John, 64, 84n35
formation, 20–21, 77, 87n114
Foucault, Michel, 5, 33n25, 33n26
freedom, 29, 37, 47–48, 55n38, 65
Freud, Sigmund, 71
frontier. *See* limitation

Geertz, Clifford, 1–2, 9n7
Genet, Jean, 66
genres, 6, 62, 71
Gilbert-Lecomte, Roger, 76
Girard, René, 84n17
Glucksmann, André, 39, 42–43, 46, 53–55
goatherds, 12
God, 12, 19, 21, 24–26, 28–29, 31–32, 37, 47, 50
gold, 30, 60, 63, 72, 74–75, 77, 82, 87n97, 88n125
Golsan, Richard J., 55n29
goodness, 13
Goodwin, James, 56n46
Green Graham, 34n54

Hamartia. *See* fault
hammer, 7, 24–26
Hegel G. W. F., 10n40, 17, 21, 28
Heidegger, Martin, 6–7, 10n39, 28, 37n101, 54n23 58n106
Heliogabalus, 65, 59, 77, 83
hermaphroditic, 74
hero, 19–20, 24, 31, 35, 41, 46, 52, 61, 63–65, 69–70
Hesiod, 19
hierarchies, 71, 81
Higgins, Kathleen M., 32n6, 38n124
Hingley, Roland, 56n66
Hoghelande, 74, 87n99
Homer, 21, 34n49, 84n11
Homoiosis. *See* resemblance
horror, 61, 65

human, 2–9, 12–16, 18–19, 21–13, 25, 31–32, 34, 40, 45, 47–48, 58, 60–65, 67, 69, 70, 72, 75, 80
Hutin, Serge. 75

idea, 3, 5, 12, 21, 23–24, 26, 42, 46–52, 55n38, 58n111, 59–63, 65, 67–72, 76, 78, 80–81, 83–85, 91
identification, 65, 69–71, 73, 81
ideology, 2, 5, 18, 25, 31, 68, 91
idol, 50
image, 19, 25–27, 29–30, 37n103, 39, 42, 49, 54n23, 55n31, 64, 68–69, 76, 78–80, 89n155, 93
indetermination, 71, 78
indifference, 5–6, 8, 14, 52–53, 60, 71, 92–93
inertia, 50, 57, 58n112, 63, 76, 92
innocent, 31, 61
instability, 63
interpretation, 4, 14, 27–28, 35n72, 37n110, 41, 43, 48, 58n111, 61, 72, 78, 85n71
intoxicating, 70
iron, 59, 72, 74, 87n97
Ivanov, Ivan. 44
Ivanov, Vyacheslav. 52, 58n107

Jackson, Robert L. 56n47
Jacobi, Friedrich H. 41, 54n15
Janicaud, Dominique. 43, 55n35–37
Johst, Hanns. 3, 9
Jung, Carl G. 75, 87n98–100
justice, 46, 62, 66

Kant, 29, 37, 37n103, 71, 77, 111
Karamazov, 28
Kaufmann, 27, 34n46
Knapp, Betina L., 87n95
Knapp, Liza, 50, 57n86
knowledge, 1, 4, 5, 9n16, 10n28, 17, 21, 27–29, 36n95, 46, 75, 86n81

Lacan, Jacques, 7, 10n38

Lacoue-Labarthe, Phillippe, 35n68, 55n26
Lampert, Laurence, 35n74
language, 1, 16, 21, 24, 41–42, 68, 70, 73–74, 79–81, 87n91, 92
law, 1, 3, 10n40, 18, 22, 27, 29, 31, 40, 58n112, 64, 67
Lawrence, D. H., 41, 54n21, 92
Lemm, Vanessa, 34n38
Lessing, G.E., 61, 69
Lévi-Stauss, 6
lie, 11, 18, 20–21, 40, 45, 49, 60, 91
life, 13–15, 17–20, 22, 25–26, 28, 30–32, 35n65, 40, 43–50, 52–53, 58n106, 59–60, 62–64, 69–70, 80–83, 86n74
light, 4–5, 7, 11, 13–14, 16, 20–21, 68, 75, 79–80
limitation, 42, 61–64, 66–67, 69, 72
lion, 25–26, 30, 37n112, 86n84
literature, 7, 10n42, 16–17, 39, 41–44, 46, 55n26, 61, 72
logos, 3–4, 67–68, 72, 80–82, 85n53, 89n148
Löwitz, Karl, 33n15
Lyotard, Jean-François, 77

madman, 21, 29
magical, 59–60, 76–77, 80, 82
magnet, 75, 77, 87n114
Mallarmé, Stéphane, 73
Mandalios, John, 33n30
mankind, 2, 20, 34n49, 48, 81
Marx, Karl, 4, 10n26
matter, 3, 21, 30, 41, 47, 63–64, 74–75, 78, 80, 82–83
Mencken H. L., 37n110
metamorphoses, 30, 61, 74–75
metaphysics, 17, 24–25, 31, 36n92, 66, 79, 83, 86n80
Middleton, 33n16
Mikhailovsky Nikolai K., 53n5
mimesis, 65, 67, 72–73, 81–83
mistake, 67
Mitleid. See pity

Mochulsky Konstantin, 56n47
modern, 2–3, 6, 8, 11–12, 14, 16–23, 25, 30–31, 40–43, 48, 55n28–29, 59, 61, 71–74, 82, 86n90
monism, 41
monotheism, 65–66
Montesquieu, 4, 10n30
morality, 3, 8, 14, 23–24, 28, 30–31, 35n65, 44, 54n18
Moses, 28–29
Müller-Lauter Wolfgand, 37n104
multiplicity, 65–66, 77
murder, 18, 22, 28–29, 44, 48–49, 70–71, 91
muthos, 61, 67, 81–82, 89n53
MyftiuBessa, 43, 55n39
mystery, 50, 77–78
mystification, 40, 72, 88
myth, 6, 19, 43, 49–51, 54n19–20, 72, 75

Nancy, Jean-Luc, 53n4
Natov, Nadine, 55n28
nature, 2, 4, 7, 9n16, 10n30, 11–18, 23–25, 27, 29, 34n51, 45, 60, 64, 72–73, 75, 77
necessity, 7, 21, 24, 42, 64
Nechaev, Sergey, 42–44, 49–50, 56n43
Nemcová, Banerjee, 56n54
Neyrat, Frédéric, 55n29
Nietzsche: *The Birth of Tragedy and Other Writings*, 11–18, 27, 36n92, 40; *Untimely Meditations*, 12, 15, 40; *Human All Too Human*, 30; *The Gay Science*, 12, 14, 18, 21–23, 26, 28–30, 35n74, 37n114, 40; *Thus Spoke Zarathustra*, 12, 18, 23–26, 29–31, 35n74, 39; *Beyond Good and Evil*, 23–24; *On The Genealogy of Morality*, 12, 14, 18–20, 23–25, 28, 35n74; *The Will to Power*, 44; *Writings from Late Notebooks*, 14
nihilism, 5–8, 15, 29, 39–47, 49–58, 71, 91–93
Nishimura, Kuniyuki, 55n29

occurrence, 66
Oedipus, 22–23, 67
opinion, 15, 25, 43, 45, 50, 57n93, 73
optimism, 11, 13–14, 17, 56n54
order, 6–7, 9, 17, 21, 24, 30–31, 41, 43, 49, 51, 59, 61–64, 66–72, 75–78, 88n129
organic, 64, 76
origin, 4, 11–12, 15, 18–19, 22–24, 27–29, 32n2, 45, 48, 59, 76, 83n3, 92
overcoming, 23–25, 45
overman, 12, 21–23, 25, 35n74,80

paideia. See education
paidia. See play
Paperno, Irina, 56n67
paradigm, 66, 78
paradoxical, 1, 8, 13, 18, 32, 41, 47–48, 65–66, 78, 81
parodia, 31
passion, 4–5, 14, 17, 45–46, 48–49, 51, 63–65, 76, 82
Patterson, Charles, 7, 19
perception, 55n38, 77
performance, 66–67, 72, 78–79, 82
pessimism, 11, 13–14, 45
phenomenon, 1, 3, 18, 28, 47, 50, 60–61, 69, 77
philanthropia, 63
Philistines, 4, 12, 15
philosophy, 7–8, 25, 39, 42–44, 62, 66–67, 71–74, 88n130
phobos. See fear, terror
pity, 61–62, 69, 82, 84n35
plague, 63–64
Plato, 3–5, 9–10, 27, 49–50, 55n35, 57n80, 61, 66–68, 70–73, 78, 80–81, 85n42,44, 86, 88n125
play, 3, 6, 9n20, 19, 21–22, 34n54, 37n116, 47, 51, 61, 64–69, 71–72, 77, 82
poetics, 62, 72–73, 77, 81, 86n90, 88n118
poetry, 42, 44, 55n26, 63, 66–67, 70, 72–73, 76–77, 80–81, 84n18, 86n87

positivism, 14
principle, 2–4, 6–7, 18, 23, 25, 40–41, 44, 47, 62, 66–67, 70, 72, 74–78, 82–83, 86n87, 93
probability, 42, 62
progress, 2–3, 12–13, 15, 18, 22, 29, 59, 64–65
prophet, 19, 29, 36n100, 40, 43, 46, 55n28, 55n32, 78
punishment, 18, 20, 46
purification, 8, 61–62, 64, 70–73, 78, 82, 84n21, 86n91, 87

Quarrel, 42–43, 67, 78

Rammstein, 93
rational, 3. 8, 39, 44, 60, 65, 67, 70, 72, 74, 80
reality, 2, 7, 27, 38n123, 46, 48, 51, 60, 62–63, 65–67, 69, 73, 75–76, 78–82, 88n136
reason, 1, 8, 15, 20, 32, 38n123, 39–40, 44–45, 49, 51–52, 56n54, 92
recognition, 41, 63
recurrence, 26, 34n51, 37n104, 46
relationship, 7, 13, 16, 25, 28–29, 34n38, 36n92, 39, 66–67
religion, 11, 32n1, 44
representation, 28, 59, 65–67, 73, 77–78, 81–83, 86n80
resemblance, 67
revelation, 7, 52, 62, 64, 70
revolt, 64, 83
revolutionary, 4, 42, 44, 66
rhetorical, 55n32, 59–60, 67
Rimbaud, Arthur, 77, 88n118
Roberts, Tyler T., 36n96
root. *See* source
Rosen, Stanley, 37n110
Rosicrucian, 74
Rotrou, Jean, 69, 85n66
rupture, 59, 63

sadism, 60
Sartarelli, Stephen, 55n29
Scanlan, James, 42, 55n30
Schopenhauer, 11, 13–14, 16–17, 27
Schutte, Ofelia, 38n124
science, 2, 14–16, 44, 50, 74
Seneca, 50, 57n90
sensibility, 68, 81
sensuous, 67–70, 72, 77–81
sentiment, 20, 60–61, 65, 76
separation, 18, 61–62, 68, 71–74, 76, 81–82
Shakespeare, 61, 71, 85n49, 86n79, 86n84
shame, 20–21, 25, 91
Shestov, 39–40, 45, 50, 53n2, 53n.4–5, 53n8, 56n48, 56n49
signification, 66, 68
simulacrum, 50, 78
Sirens, 60–62, 65
slaughter, 7, 15, 18–19, 34n38, 60, 64, 93
Socrates, 3–4, 9, 15, 43, 66, 72, 80–81
Soll, Ivan, 13, 32n9
Sophocles, 6, 10n36, 10n37, 66
soul, 18, 21, 33n33, 47, 64, 67, 72–73, 75
source, 7–8, 14, 18–19, 21, 25, 41, 44, 51, 62, 66, 72, 81, 87n95
spectacle, 21, 60–63, 65, 67–69, 71, 73, 76–82
spectator, 21, 59, 61, 65, 67–69, 71, 81, 91
Sperber, Julius, 74, 87n101
spirit, 13, 19–22, 25–26, 29–31, 37n104, 37n105, 37n107, 37n110, 39–40, 53n6, 55n38, 56n60, 70, 74–80, 82–83
stage, 11, 20, 22, 61–62, 66–68, 73–74, 77, 79, 81–82, 85n54
Steiner, George, 53n2
stone, 25–26, 49, 75
sublime, 16, 25, 64–65, 77–78, 82
substance, 7, 74
suffering, 5, 14, 23, 29, 34n51, 39, 53n5, 60–61, 82
suicide, 46–48, 51–53, 58n112

supremacy, 83
Swift, 4–5
Synaesthesia. See aesthetic
synthetic, 76

Tabucchi, Antonio, 7, 10n42
telos, 61, 75, 80
terror, 6, 21–22, 62, 65, 82
theater, 59, 61–65, 67–73, 76–79, 81–88, 91
thought, 3, 5, 8, 10–11, 13–14, 23–24, 28, 31, 34n51, 39, 41–41, 46–49, 52–54, 60, 71–73, 75–76, 83, 57n91, 91–92
Tonelli, Franco, 62, 84n21, 87n91
torture, 19, 60, 70, 88n118
tradition, 2, 9n7, 11, 14, 19, 28–30, 37n110, 41, 43, 71, 73–76, 80–82, 86n91
tragedy, 6, 12, 15, 26–28, 30, 39, 49, 57n71, 61, 67, 84n16
transcendental, 28, 60
transfiguration, 64, 71, 78, 88n126
transformation, 14, 21, 27, 30, 69, 71, 75–76, 78, 80, 82
transmutation, 74–77, 80
truth, vii, 14, 16, 24–25, 31, 37n103, 39, 43, 45, 50, 52, 53n5, 70, 78, 89n140
Turgenev, Ivan, 44
Tylor, E.B., 1, 8n2, 12
tyrant, 21, 23

Ulysses, 60, 62, 71, 85n49
uncanny, 7, 60
unfulfilled, 64
unification, 74–77
universe, 62, 74–77
univocal, 40, 41, 44

uselessness, 73, 80–81

Valentino, Russell S., 55n32
Valéry, 73, 80, 86n90
value, 1, 4, 6, 13–14, 19–20, 23–24, 30–31, 55n28, 60, 65, 71
valuelessness, 40–41
Varro, 82
verisimilitude. *See* probability
vices, 64
violence, 5, 10n40, 13, 21, 24, 66, 71, 81, 83, 86n77, 91–92, 93n1
virtues, 23
Visvanathan, Shiv, 19
Vonnegut, Kurt, 92, 93n2

Weber, Max, 2
Weisse, Christian F., 61
Welles, Orson, 22
West, (ern)19, 29, 40, 42, 50, 59, 66, 67, 71–72, 74, 76, 80–81, 86n80, 92
Wiesel, Eli, 92
will, 16, 19, 25–26, 30, 46–47, 52–53, 58n106 n111, 64
wisdom, 16, 25–27, 60, 75
Wittgenstein, Ludwig, 73
words, 1, 5–7, 12, 18, 24, 28–30, 36n92, 48, 51, 57n75, 59, 68, 71, 76, 79–81, 91
world, 3–6, 8, 10, 12, 14–17, 25, 28, 31, 40, 42, 45, 47–48, 50, 52, 61–62, 64, 66–71, 74–77, 80–81, 92

Yeats, W. B., 73, 80

Zarathustra, 5, 12, 21, 23–26, 29–31, 35n68 n74

About the Author

Max Statkiewicz is a Professor Emeritus at the University of Wisconsin-Madison. He is working in the domain of classical literature and philosophy and theory of literature. He is the author of numerous articles and the book *Rhapsody of Philosophy*, about the recent interpretations of Plato's thought. He has translated many essays from French, German, and Russian as well as the book of Ulrike Oudée Dünkelsbühler, *Kritik der Rahmen-Vernunft: Parergon-Versionen nach Kant und Derrida*.

www.ingramcontent.com/pod-product-compliance
Lightning Source LLC
Chambersburg PA
CBHW020127010526
44115CB00008B/1015